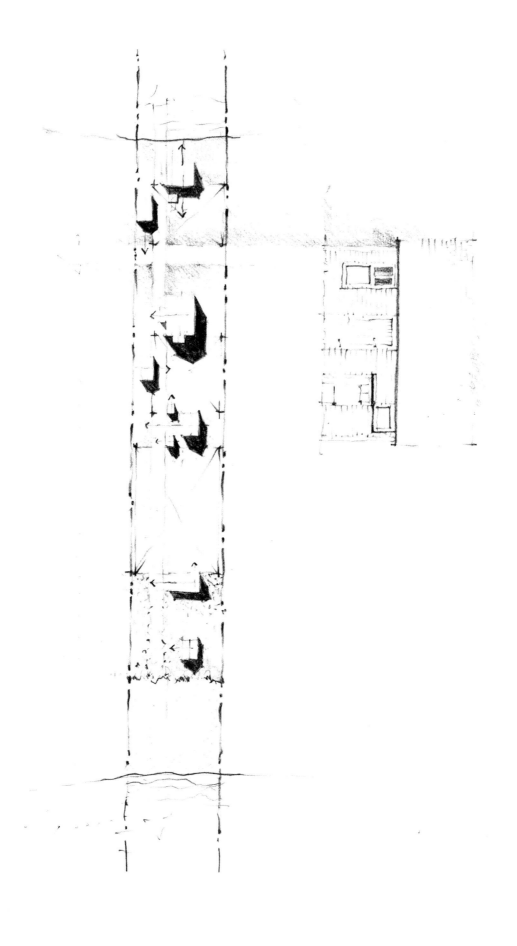

Plain Modern
The Architecture of Brian MacKay-Lyons

Malcolm Quantrill

With contributions by Glenn Murcutt and Kenneth Frampton
and project texts by Brian MacKay-Lyons

FOR AMY

Brian   29.3.06

Graham Foundation for Advanced Studies in the Fine Arts, Chicago

Princeton Architectural Press, New York

Graham Foundation/Princeton Architectural Press series

New Voices in Architecture

presents first monographs on emerging designers from around the world

Published by

Princeton Architectural Press

37 East Seventh Street

New York, New York 10003

For a free catalog of books, call 1.800.722.6657.

Visit our web site at www.papress.com.

Publication of this book has been supported by a grant from the
Graham Foundation for Advanced Studies in the Fine Arts.

Images for publication were acquired with the help of a grant from the
Canada Council for the Arts.

Canada Council   Conseil des Arts
for the Arts   du Canada

Editor: Nancy Eklund Later

Designer: Jan Haux

Publisher's acknowledgments: special thanks to Nettie Aljian, Dorothy Ball, Nicola
Bednarek, Janet Behning, Megan Carey, Penny (Yuen Pik) Chu, Russell Fernandez,
Clare Jacobson, Mark Lamster, Linda Lee, Katharine Myers, Lauren Nelson, Molly
Rouzie, Jane Sheinman, Scott Tennent, Jennifer Thompson, Paul G. Wagner, Joseph
Weston, and Deb Wood of Princeton Architectural Press —Kevin C. Lippert, publisher

Library of Congress Cataloging-in-Publication Data

Quantrill, Malcolm, 1931–

Plain modern : the architecture of Brian Mackay-Lyons / Malcolm Quantrill ; with contributions by Glenn Murcutt and Kenneth Frampton ; and project texts by Brian MacKay-
Lyons.—1st ed.

p. cm.— (New voices in architecture)

SBN 1-56898-477-4 (alk. paper)

1. MacKay-Lyons, Brian. 2. Architecture—Nova Scotia—20th century. I. Murcutt, Glenn.
II. Frampton, Kenneth. III. MacKay-Lyons, Brian. IV. Graham Foundation for Advanced
Studies in the Fine Arts. V. Title. VI. Series.

NA749.M317A4 2005

720'.92—dc22

2005007019

CONTENTS

This book is dedicated to my family, both near and far: to Esther, Francesca and Jason, and Alexandra, and to Christopher, Jan and Rani, and to Max and Arne.

Foreword

My knowledge of the work of Brian MacKay-Lyons came around 1985, when a fellow Australian architect brought it to my attention through international architectural publications. In 1987 Brian and his wife Marilyn visited me in Sydney. Since then we have met several times, and in 2001 I had the privilege of spending time with them in their native Nova Scotia, visiting urban and coastal buildings and ending up at their extraordinary coastal farm, site of the Ghost Laboratory projects conducted with students of architecture. This visit made for my understanding of the integration of Brian's work to place, technology, and the maritime culture of his region. In 2003 we met again whilst both of us were visiting professors at the University of Michigan, Ann Arbor, and having visited him on Nova Scotia's Atlantic coast, the site of his project with the students, I was in a position to fully understand the work from that studio.

Canada has had European settlement for four hundred years, yet much of the coast that I visited remains densely forested, providing at times a dark, monolithic, impenetrable barrier, where sites often feel carved out from the enclosing forest density. There are also many coastal environments where large, gray, worn rocks line the shores and keep the forests at bay, providing superb zones between the forests and the coastal and estuarine waters.

In Nova Scotia, where temperatures fluctuate frequently and dramatically above and below zero, the climate can be extremely tough and particularly so on buildings. Combined with the effects of alternating rain and sunshine, the durability of materials and detailing are fully tested. Vernacular buildings inform us about how well various materials perform, and here MacKay-Lyons draws much of his knowledge through observation of the local building culture.

The traditional buildings, particularly those associated with fishing and lobster harvesting, are constructed with tight, crisp, timber-clad skins over simple, internal, exposed structure. This results in strong geometric forms that, over time, weather like the coastal landscape to grays and silver grays. These buildings are tough and direct where their forms connect the land to the waterways. They often open on two sides, forming a through-space in their core that allows the landscape to continue unimpeded between their solid timber walls. These buildings inform many of MacKay-Lyons's works, which in turn reveal and amplify the cultural and natural structure of the coastal landscape.

Much is being discussed today on the subject of ecologically responsive buildings, and none represent a better example than the timber buildings of Nova Scotia. Here they are constructed somewhat like boats, their timber cladding fixed to lightweight framing. A minimum volume of material, derived from economic, renewable resources, is consumed. This regional construction method has influenced the thinking of MacKay-Lyons, rendering the work affordable, low-tech, tough, and absolutely modern.

The architecture of Brian MacKay-Lyons shows clarity in planning, resulting in forms that are direct, simple, and elegant. The buildings are beautifully sited and crafted. This is an honest, no-nonsense architecture that avoids the fashions of the day. It exhibits that rare quality—authenticity.

Glenn Murcutt

Preface

This is a book about a rather special kind of architecture, about the original and highly provocative forms of dwelling currently being added to the modernist canon by Nova Scotia native Brian MacKay-Lyons. The correctness of describing these unique structures with the term "architecture" might be disputed by some who align themselves with Nikolaus Pevsner's suggestion that only cathedrals and similar monuments constitute *Baukunst* ("the art of building"). Unembellished constructions such as MacKay-Lyons's would fall into the category of "mere building." Extending this cunning but fallacious argument, Denis Hollier, a professor of French at Yale University, writes in his *Against Architecture: The Writings of Georges Bataille*:

> The "jobs" taken on by the word "architecture" certainly have more import than its meaning. When architecture is discussed it is never simply a question of architecture; the metaphors cropping up as a result of these jobs are almost inseparable from the proper meaning of the term. The proper meaning itself remains somehow indeterminate.... Architecture refers to whatever there is in an edifice that cannot be reduced to mere building. Whatever allows a construction to escape from purely utilitarian concerns, whatever is aesthetic about it. This encroachment by an irreducibly metaphorical situation, with architecture defined as the representation of something else, extends to language, where architectural metaphors are very common.... Never mind if the proper meaning of architecture remains subject to discussion. What is essential is that it always does its job. No metaphor is innocent, and the less it is contrived the less it is innocent.

In the face of so much Yale-style rhetoric I can hardly hope to argue successfully for the retention of my own architectural innocence, nor for that of my subject. I have been privileged to work very closely with MacKay-Lyons, benefiting from his willingness to share his ideas and thoughts with me during a number of meetings held over the course of four years. Together we have explored the metaphors, or "representations," embedded in his work. Here, in the following pages, I have attempted to share what makes the architect tick, to elucidate his approaches to the art and science of building design.

Previously, between 1974 and the early 1990s, I had enjoyed a similar collaboration with Reima Pietilä. I first met the Finnish master architect in 1960, when I was working in the Helsinki office of Aarne Ervi. He became a very close friend and also a staunch supporter of my efforts to understand Finnish modernism, which has consumed the better part of my forty-year career as a historian, critic, and educator. In the course of our collaboration he shared many of his most profound thoughts with me. Although he was, by the mid-1970s, an extremely successful architect, well known internationally, with work in India and Kuwait as well as Finland, there was nothing of the high and mighty about him. The openness and accessibility he possessed came from his being a natural egalitarian, whose first inclination was to share his insights with those he judged to be fellow oarsmen in what he called the "Ark of Architecture."

What I succeeded in doing in the case of Pietilä was to get inside the architect's head, to connect with what he was thinking, saying, and doing. From that advantageous position—close to his brain-box, as it were—I was able to interpret his intentions, even though what he thought and said would normally have been quite outside my knowledge and experience. The book that emerged from this collaboration reflects the intimate nature of our relationship. Pietilä always maintained that "in the case of architecture, the architect is always the object," rather than the subject, of enquiry. From that viewpoint, Pietilä was an ideal "object."

Since that time, I had simply not come across another *Baukunstler* ("building artist") with whom I felt comfortable traveling on the Ark of Architecture. When I made Brian's acquaintance in early February 2000, I almost immediately began to compare our spontaneous conversations to those I had shared with Pietilä, as images of a peasant prince among a bloated bourgeoisie, a gypsy baron capable of outmaneuvering the pompous landlords, once again came to mind. While he is a very civilized human being, I have to admit that Brian is also something else: here is an obviously original architect who is, at the same time, a natural-born teacher, no doubt partly because of his nonconformist character and the way his work "preaches" his message. I had invited him to give a lecture to my students at Texas A+M University, and his radical approach resulted in a most memorable evening. There was the preacher, down among the student "congregation," literally slugging out his text—"How the Virtues of Architecture Can Overcome the Evils of Ignorance and Malpractice."

I was impressed by the clarity of Brian's thinking and the facility with which he communicated to those around him. These qualities were combined with the accessibility of his own design ideas. It soon seemed obvious that I would benefit enormously if I could engage MacKay-Lyons's interest in acting as my fellow traveler. I had once again become intrigued by the possibility of getting inside an architect's head.

I was interested in taking the wraps off the architect and presenting the person, his ideas, and his work in book form, but a form that was essentially free from the conventions of an architectural monograph. This would involve the exploration of the physical nature of Brian's architecture as well as the delineation of its symbolic and cultural values. In other words, I wanted to invoke Pietilä's category of the object in order to establish an inside track where the innermost thoughts and the visible endeavors of the architect are laid open to the scrutiny and questioning of the critic.

From the beginning, Brian and I understood that our working together involved, and depended upon, our belief that the explorations we proposed and the discoveries we made were but a continuation of our own professional studies in architecture. As we set out on this voyage, we had Brian's work always at our elbow; nevertheless, we were never very far from more general architectural considerations. We began to map architectural design as a special kind of adventure in its own right. Such an adventure, which quite often requires travel over unknown terrain, demands integrity, resilience, and a certain recklessness of spirit. "That's where you come in, Brian," I quipped, "with your ability to stand on (what Browning called) the 'dangerous edge of things.'" He answered me smartly, "I take it you mean to place me at that essential frontier of the intellectual landscape?" On the evidence it would seem to be perfectly unreasonable to deny him this expectation.

I am an Englishman by birth and an architect by profession. I was born and raised in the County of Norfolk, in the great cathedral city of Norwich. A veritable museum of architecture, within its Roman walls resides a superb collection of Romanesque, Gothic, and Georgian buildings. Norwich is sited on low-lying riverside terrain at the heart of that great bump on the lower–right-hand side of England's profile. That bump contains the extended territory of East Anglia, a region renowned for its agriculture and fishing. Today it is still less accessible by rail and road than most of England.

This flat, low-lying Norfolk landscape, with its sandy shores and piney woodlands, the gentle lapping of the North Sea in summer and the majestic crashing of its waves in winter, became an essential part of my environmental memory. Such landscapes would remain permanent and vital touchstones for my subsequent life in architecture. By the mid-1950s I had discovered the Baltic coast of southern Finland, while searching for Finnish modern architecture. Wandering also barefoot along the beach of Gdansk at night, I felt at home as the fine sand sifted between my toes.

In the sculpted land forms of Nova Scotia we have the crest and hollow upon which architecture sits and gestures; the coastline that juts up suddenly into an array of hostile cliffs, or dips and slips away to vanish in the receding sea. And in its unfolding, we witness a church, some houses, perhaps even a chance inn, surfacing beyond a flourish of wind-swept woods. A sudden undulation before us, a mere bump in the ground, is enough cause to gather settling folk, their enclosing walls shaping the pre-ordained spot, gradually, into the distinctive massing of community within the impregnated landscape.

In Norfolk we wander along the edges of the coastline and squat down to come into closer proximity with the ocean. We are held back by one physical barrier or another: either a threatening wall of overhanging cliffs or the receding, bubbling edge of the sea itself. Finland offered me, instead, stress-free passage to the water. In the archipelago, where the landmass caresses the ocean with an array of neat gardens, shining new slip-ways, and quaint, brightly painted summer bungalows, the onlooker can slip a hand into the Baltic, sifting through the chilled water with near-frozen fingers. It gives a frisson. In this way both the remote, impenetrable mysteries of Finnish culture and the symbolic depths of its architecture are offset by the immediacy of an awakening.

While water is not something one can readily get a grip on, it certainly stands in for a positive dose of environmental reality. Although the Norfolk coastline does not afford this kind of reassurance, it may certainly be found elsewhere. Moving the seat of my enquiries from Finland to Kingsburg, I now stretch out my arm and immerse my hand in the Atlantic Ocean, on hospitable shelves afforded by Nova Scotia's coastal plains.

Malcolm Quantrill

Acknowledgments

This study was effectively initiated by Professor Tom McKittrick who, as head of the Department of Architecture at Texas A+M University, invited Brian MacKay-Lyons to be our Thomas Bullock Visiting Professor of Architecture in spring 2000. I was thus able to get to know Brian at first hand. Our current department head, Dr. Phillip Tabb, AIA, has supported my research in Canada through his generous attitude toward the travel leave necessary for this project. The annual bursary I receive as a Distinguished Professor of Texas A+M University has helped substantially in meeting my research costs.

By the summer of 2002, when Brian gave me permission to write this book, I had still not negotiated a contract with an appropriate publisher. It was at this point that my friend and longtime collaborator, Professor Stanford Anderson of the Massachusetts Institute of Technology, suggested that I approach Princeton Architectural Press through one of its editors, Nancy Eklund Later. Nancy became an immediate and enthusiastic supporter of this work, guiding me through minefields that resulted from my determination to create an innovative text, one that would offer an adequate accompaniment to MacKay-Lyons's highly original and provocative architecture. Charting new courses runs the risk of throwing a vessel off-course, but with Nancy at the helm I never doubted that we would reach safe harbor.

Brian gave generously of his time, both in his office and at home on his Kingsburg farm in Nova Scotia, and my research centered on our dialogues. In the office we were supported by the close professional collaboration of Chad Jamieson, one of Brian's young assistants, and by the rapid-fire responses of Constance Gould, his ever-resourceful office administrator. On the farm and in the surrounding countryside, we were always welcomed by Brian's wife, Marilyn, who provided both good food and ready good humor.

Over the past three years I have paid half-a-dozen visits to Nova Scotia to meet with Brian, his staff, and his clients, resulting in illuminating conversations about the work and the Nova Scotia landscape. So far my dear wife, Esther, has not been up there once, on the Canadian East Coast I have come to love, and I must thank her for her tolerance and forbearance while she has kept herself and our Texas homestead cool down here in the blistering heat of the Brazos Bottom.

Malcolm Quantrill

It is an honor for the work of my practice to be placed in the larger architectural discourse by such a distinguished author as Malcolm Quantrill. His insightful ideas immediately intrigued me, and throughout the process of making this book we have become fellow travelers on the road of architectural investigation, discovering shared values. His wit has put a smile on my face.

I thank my friend and mentor Glenn Murcutt for his foreword. His clarity and integrity have influenced my work deeply, and his practice has served as a model for all of us practicing outside the centers of fashion. Thanks also go to Kenneth Frampton for his essay on the Ghost Lab. His articulation of the idea of critical regionalism has reinforced my belief in the importance of place as a source of content. I also owe a lasting debt of gratitude to Charles Moore, whose inspiration as my mentor and teacher continues to guide my work.

I am indebted to Richard Solomon and to the Graham Foundation for their generous support of this book, as well as to the Canada Council for the Arts for its grant used to acquire photographs. I extend my thanks to Kevin Lippert of Princeton Architectural Press for believing in this project and assigning top-quality professionals to it. In particular, our editor Nancy Eklund Later has brought real intellectual engagement to the book well beyond her role in managing the process, and we are fortunate to have had the opportunity to work with graphic designer Jan Haux.

My colleagues in the practice generously tolerated my distraction from day-to-day work that comes with a project such as this. Constance Gould, my office manager, knows firsthand about its effect on a small business. Staff architect Chad Jamieson has led the office effort on the book with professional discipline. Talbot Sweetapple has made a significant contribution to the work presented here and will have an even more significant role going forward as a principal of MacKay-Lyons Sweetapple Architects.

Ultimately, it is my wife, Marilyn, who has been the greatest patron of my practice. I am unbelievably fortunate to have her unconditional support. A sustainable practice is an extension of a life in balance.

Brian MacKay-Lyons

Plain Modern:
The Architecture of Brian MacKay-Lyons
Malcolm Quantrill

He strides across the field lying next to his farmstead home. His athletic frame moves quickly, his legs gently pressing into the softly undulating terrain. Hatless, his bald head flashes in the sunlight, like a beacon to guide me on this, my first visit to Kingsburg. He could be a farmer, except that his arms do not thrash as he walks: he's carrying something to keep them pinned to his sides. This man, informal and quite approachable—even friendly, on closer acquaintance—combines poet and peasant in the same single being. Make no mistake about it, he is truly a peasant in the best sense—a worthy, yeoman, salt-of-the-earth type. For many architects, such sense of savor has escaped from their taste buds long before they might learn to suck the salt from a briny finger.

MacKay-Lyons is certainly not one of those generic, common, or garden-variety North American peasants: he is 100 percent Acadian. There is nothing of the city slicker in this proud, unrepentant Canadian. When he comes on stage, both the poet and peasant are immediately evident in his attitude, his sense of purpose. As he crosses the field of constructional endeavor, he sets about making memorials out of what seems barely memorable, in the wilder, more abandoned stretches of Nova Scotia, where it is not quite clear what is land and what is water. For Nova Scotians, balanced precariously on an exposed rim of the Atlantic Ocean, occupy unique geographical tracts, caught between the inhospitable earth beneath and occasional glimpses of the heavens overhead. Poised "between the devil and the deep," they endeavor to come to terms with their insecurity, with their condition of being "without foundation."

In Nova Scotia, one is reminded of Browning's "dangerous edge of things," a sense of instability, of an unsure foothold on the sand, of indeterminacy, of being without benefit of the benchmarks of history, having only ephemeral watermarks of tides or the sound of falling trees to serve as nature's ruthless and rootless clock. All this breeds a determination to convert the instability of *being* into security and stability for their particular way of life; into Heidegger's sense of *dwelling*. Brian MacKay-Lyons is poised on this "dangerous edge," struggling to balance the elements that shape the geological profile of an Atlantic coastline with the elements of architecture—in his case, a modern architecture that is bold enough to tell the plain truth of its materiality, to stand on his native soil in modern terms, an art form that he sows and grows on those crests and hollows, cultivating his crop of *Baukunst* from the ground up.

As we leave the farmhouse, Brian goes on ahead to beat a path. Now he is maybe thirty yards in front of me, having almost reached the brow of the field's tree-crowned crest. "Almost there," he booms, as he waves me on. Two minutes later I'm standing by the architect's side. "See," he says, commanding my attention with his outstretched arm. His finger points emphatically down to the roof of an attenuated, wedge-shaped form that floats in the landscape beneath us. "There she blows: Messenger II." I have just a couple of minutes to assess the size and shape of the vessel moored below us before we turn on our heels in the rough turf and clamber down the slope to arrive in direct confrontation with "Messenger II."

There is very little resemblance between the taut coastal terrain of Nova Scotia and the rolling landscape of Palladio's Veneto, but because I recently returned from Venice, where Andrea's villas impressed themselves upon my imagination with renewed clarity, the more immediate images of ships quickly fade from my mind. In their place, the Palladian villa appears, and I begin to wonder whether, in the conceptual sense, Brian's architecture might be related. Perhaps. Objects in the landscape, his houses on the Nova Scotia coast literally serve as its landmarks, giving well-marked identity to the placelessness of place.

When I looked closely at the gaping hole that opens up the ocean side of Messenger House II and found a covered terrace from which one can look out to sea, I again asked myself, "Could this be further evidence of a Palladian motif?" For what I saw, and what I instinctively felt as I surveyed this expansive and as yet unfinished vantage point, suggested one of Palladio's common devices, an architectural feature invented precisely for this particular purpose. Brian has told me repeatedly of the importance to him of historical examples, of theory based on precedent, and of the necessity of making reference to the cultural evolution of architecture. I tell him, "You have given new life to Palladio's recessed portico. Not with the splendor of the Villa Cornaro, perhaps, or even that of the Villa Pisani, but something like the down-to-earth version we find in the more modest Villa Poiana."

The owner of the house, the former grammar school headmaster John Messenger, seemed very happy with the progress on his house so far. He tells me:

> *I guess it's just what you might expect. Brian has used most of this side of the house to frame a view down toward the sea. Yet the way he's done it brings us an experience that's totally unexpected. It's quite a remarkable feat. Here we are, more or less at ground level on the Nova Scotia coast. But Brian has combined a slight elevation of the deck above the natural slope of the land down to the sea, with the effect of some grand villa in the Veneto. The result is that, when it's finished, we'll enjoy a view from an upper floor, the* piano nobile *itself.*

Although sharing traits with Palladio's ideal, MacKay-Lyons's is a distinctly modern architecture. But I would not have thought of labeling his architecture as "plain modern" if it hadn't been for an important encounter with another outstanding modern architect, in the summer of 2001.

It was not in Italy, however, that I made the most direct and appropriate connection to Brian's Nova Scotia houses. Finding myself in Oporto, Portugal, with time on my hands, I decided to telephone Álvaro Siza and ask if he would let me visit him in his studio. I originally met Siza in Finland the year he received the Alvar Aalto Medal, although I doubted that he would remember that encounter. He told me, however, that he was familiar with my books about Finnish architecture, and he invited me to meet with him the following afternoon. As a result I spent two hours in the esteemed Portuguese architect's company.

In the taxi on my way to Siza's studio, I began to ask myself what on earth we would talk about and just how would I get to know Siza at close quarters. At that time I knew very little about modern Portuguese architecture in general or Siza's own work in particular. Of course, I had visited a number of his buildings in and around Oporto, but since I didn't know these works well they didn't seem to offer much of a promise for fruitful conversation.

I recalled one of my favorite books on architecture, George Kubler's *Portuguese Plain Architecture, 1521–1706*, and its examination of a very restrained type of work by Portuguese architects characterized by clarity, order, proportion, and simplicity. In

the early moments of my meeting with Siza, I dared to suggest that through the example of his own contemporary work we were witnessing a rebirth of Portuguese plain architecture. Appreciative of this comparison, Siza and I spent most our time together discussing the importance of plainness, rather than decoration, in the history of architectural culture. I well remember Siza's concluding comments:

> *Plainness is no accident in good architecture. You have only to think of Karnak, the Parthenon, and those marvelous Romanesque abbeys in France. Portuguese plain is part of a great tradition, part of a recurring theme, which is simply a cultural resistance to unnecessary elaboration and embellishment.*

Through this completely accidental conversation with the Portuguese master, the common ground between MacKay-Lyons's modernist aesthetic and that of Portuguese plain architecture came into focus on a midsummer afternoon. Siza's insistence that "Plainness is no accident in good architecture" seemed to fix Brian's contribution securely in place. Here is a modern architect designing and building in the shadow of postmodernism, and yet he still manages to mine a genuine vein of modernism three-quarters of a century after the movement's original high season. He is taking the raw material of modernism, refining it, and bringing it to an elegant simplicity in the ultimate splendor of plainness.

I had previously observed that if, within a culture, the art of building is passed from generation to generation, then we have something called an "established tradition"; and so long as such a tradition is in effect, there is no need for a conceptual theory to reinforce the processing of planning, spatial organization, and construction. This observation interested Brian, as it offered absolute ratification of his own "grassroots" theory of architectural production. On Sunday morning, as we were opening up our conversation, he said there was something about the notion of an architecture without theory that had two quite opposite appeals. On the one hand, it struck him as being essentially organic, while on the other, it sounded "quite hazardous."

Architectural form provides for the demonstration of its substance and appearance within two necessarily distinct and contrasting categories. It would either conform to the rigid, puritanical, minimalist, and static character of "a box," or it would possess an interpretive freedom associated with, say, a musical instrument, which is capable of being tuned and therefore includes potentially variable results. An architecture as an "instrument," rather than as a predetermined formal or geometric entity, would be open to the possibility of free interpretation or free performance. Brian says, "I'm not quite sure about the limitations of your definition of categories. If you look at it from my point of view, I have a hunch that you might need a third category for what I do. Maybe you should include my things in a separate, in-between category of objects." Brian pauses, before he suggests, "Why don't you just put me down as a maker of 'well-tuned boxes'?" This hybrid classification fits comfortably into my overall view of his experiments, of the production of an architecture that is essentially plain modern. Brian continues to muse, "Maybe that's it. You know, like Bach's well-tempered clavier, or Reyner Banham's well-tempered environment? Maybe what we should also be talking about is the case for Brian's well-tempered box?"

Since Brian is enthusiastic about the inclusiveness of sources and influences in the design process, I ask him to tell me what some of those stimuli might be. In other words, "How could the box cease to be a box and adopt a more responsive *being*?" "Well, first of all, there's the landscape," he answers.

> *That plays a big part. Architecture has to nestle down into it, or stand up and be counted. It's like you said about Palladio—although in his case he mostly makes his buildings sit up and attract attention. That's the main idea in the classical landscape. If you have a virtue, if there's absolutely no doubt about the virtue of a particular architecture, then you should display it boldly for all to see. Make sure it sits up. Be sure it's on view.*

He stops abruptly to change direction. "It's different here in the New World. There's too much puritanical sentiment still thriving in the North American environment."

Does that mean you have to keep your virtue under wraps? "Architecture under wraps?" he laughs. "Is that plausible?" Pausing first, Brian concludes, "I say yes, because some people don't much care for architects. Even worse, my friend, there are a lot of people out there who absolutely hate architecture."

I had been talking to Brian for some time about the Halifax Shipyard. I had questioned whether the imagery of shipbuilding had any effect on his design concept. The jury may still be out on that issue, but what I found when I went to the Halifax Shipyard was absolutely extraordinary. It was my very first experience of a shipyard, and I was totally unprepared for a complete change from our normal human and architectural scale to a truly overwhelming monumentality.

It struck me that I was being drawn into the experiences of Jonathan Swift's Gulliver, but in reverse. There I was, relatively tiny and insignificant, in the presence of colossal pieces of machinery, of ships revealing their whole depth and volume instead of the comparatively small portion we are accustomed to seeing above water. Only slowly, as I wandered around the shipyard, did I begin to piece together some possible explanations for this mysterious condition of space and form. I came to realize that it was not only a change of scale I was trying to accommodate; the geometry of the shipyard was also strangely unfamiliar. It was as though someone were trying to break the rules of perspective by reorganizing and re-presenting the objects within a composition.

The inherent success of Brian's work stems in part from his desire to revive the spirit of the shipbuilding industry in Nova Scotia. By incorporating into his architecture some of its forms, images, and materials, he recalls the workings of the shipyard and its haunting presence in the town, imprinting a sort of residual memory of

shipbuilding in the expression of his own landlocked inventions. There is a constructional link between the shipyard ethos and Brian's own fabrications. What he is making today has a clearly defined relationship to what was made in Halifax during much of the twentieth century. The production of the Nova Scotia shipyard was quite inseparable from the essential processes of early modernism.

In one way—in basic formal terms—MacKay-Lyons's work might be described as combining and confusing the traditions and languages of both barn and boat. Within the context of Nova Scotia, this appears to reveal an ethical function for an architecture that is designed to fit a land whose poetic is framed by a hostile sea and seemingly interminable pine forests, whose coastal stretches once embraced prosperous centers of manufacture and world trade.

Today this land is a haven more for the adventurous tourist than for a global economy. Such a paradigm shift in a culture cries out for an attitude of determined resistance in the region's architecture. This is precisely the kind resistance that MacKay-Lyons infuses into the fabric of his buildings. His plain modern is not a style but a philosophical attitude. It is a determined approach that resists the counter-culture of tourism and its insidious companion, popular magazine imagery. The primary intention of MacKay-Lyons's approach to design is centered on bringing the isolated province of Nova Scotia into the center of the modern world. This he achieves in part by incorporating the clear-cut craft of twentieth-century shipbuilding into the no-nonsense plainness of his own modern architecture.

Brian resists the tendency of postmodernism and its absorption in the superficiality of a "photo-journalese" culture. We may therefore define his plain modern design path as one seeking to attain the objectives of a truly ethical approach to making architecture.

At first glance his work might seem to echo Frank Stella's sentiment, "What you see is what you get." But, in contrast to Stella, Brian has a view of *Baukunst* that actually includes the incorporation of meaning. He sets out to make meaningful statements in the contexts of landscape or townscape. His statements are accessible to the public at large as part of his effort to shape and articulate a common ethos. His philosophy doesn't need a score of commentators to interpret it for the common man. The strength of Brian's statements are that they say what they mean. Among its other attributes, therefore, MacKay-Lyons's architecture helps to ensure that its underlying message is not likely to become lost in translation.

In *The Ethical Function of Architecture*, Karsten Harries proposed that the function of architecture should be that of "helping to articulate a common ethos." A resulting ethical architecture would have to be conceived and operate *beyond* conventional, academic, and other regulated formal constraints. In allowing for and seeking to accommodate an architecture that is beyond previously accepted conventions, we would have to abandon, at the same time, the notion of architecture as a realm of exclusive gestures or intentions, or what we typically mean when we stray into the terrain of *meaning*. In other words, the practice of architecture would be freed of constraints imposed by an elitist education that is intent on planting in young minds a body of concepts derived from so-called "informed taste" and other cultural limitations. Like Chaucer's *Canterbury Tales*, written in the English vernacular of its day (rather than in Latin), this inclusive architecture might exert the sway it once held during both the European Middle Ages and the Italian Renaissance. History has clearly revealed the capacity of architecture for rising to the occasion in expressing and representing the groundswell of social and cultural thought. Without such stimuli, *Baukunst* lacks the wherewithall to act as a continuing and progressive framework of human endeavor. As MacKay-Lyons is fond of noting, "In order to be truly comprehensible, architecture has to demonstrate a clarity that makes it sufficiently democratic, as to be accessible to an educated public."

The salient articles of Brian MacKay-Lyons's faith are contained in his explanation of the "Three Fs for an Architecture of Regionalism": fitting, framing, and forming. The architect has elaborated on the operation of these keywords in his approach to the design task and its realization.

FITTING, in MacKay-Lyons's philosophy, has fundamentally to do with the process by which an architectural idea seeks to locate itself within the exploration and development of the site; how that idea searches for appropriate strategies to permit the placement of its program within a prescribed terrain; and finally, how the idea achieves its initial design objectives by showing in turn how it accommodates the salient characteristics of the landscape. In Heidegger's sense, we could say that by fitting an idea to a site, the *being* of that idea realizes its condition of *dwelling* in relation to a particular place.

FRAMING, for MacKay-Lyons, has to do with the strategy of *Bauen* ("building") through the realization of a design idea by means of construction. The idea that is fitted to the site exists as some form of skeletal exploration of space.

Brian's explorations could be likened to those fantastic domestic constructions by Dubuffet found in his book *Edifices*. The maisons Dubuffet models mostly have only interior "outlines" of spaces, only internal walls and stairways. In this way Dubuffet leaves the final shape of his maisons open to interpretation. The artist's programs for domestic habitation are, thus, absolutely opposed to those prescribed by, say, Le Corbusier. In his iconic Maison Domino, the external form is clearly defined by the edge conditions of its floor slabs; as a consequence, there is no accommodation of free and expansive form in the architect's domestic formula.

In contrast, Dubuffet's "edifices" suggest space and freedom to accommodate terraces, balconies, and other indoor/outdoor delights around the periphery of the structure's core (note the irony of the artist's title in relation to a collection of structures that, for the most part, lacks any trace of those very edifices). In fact, the suggestion seems to be that within this freedom to complete the "design," the viewer is actually free to invent and add a personal interpretation of the structure's missing parts, searching experimentally for the conclusive envelope of an edifice.

Consistent with his paintings and sculpture, Dubuffet's maisons are distinctly open-ended works. MacKay-Lyons is undoubtedly a supporter of Dubuffet's frameworks: while his forms may be generated by framing, Brian's aim is to avoid any restrictive predetermination of final external form. While the framing of Brian's buildings, particularly the houses, may contribute substantially to the forming of those structures, it is the idea of fitting the work into the context that remains the dominant influence in shaping the finished product.

Forming is MacKay-Lyons's term for "giving shape to an idea." But since the idea, the notional concept, is born from the shape of the site, this means that the forming or shaping of that idea is a marriage between the sensitivity of the architect and the landscape features of the site; an act of affection for the nature of the materials within the manifestation of a particular, local groundswell.

The master Finnish architect Reima Pietilä consistently advocated that in architecture the *idea* has a separate existence from that of the *form* and that the *idea* must therefore possess the energy to survive and outlive any distorted representation of its essence. He believed that the idea was in constant danger of being diluted, or "inadequately translated," during the design development process. The test of an idea's strength is, perhaps, comparable to the German concept related to the capacity of a wine to be exported outside its region of origin and production, without loss of quality or character: this characteristic is called *Öchsle* in German, or "ox-strength."

Implicit in Pietilä's idea-versus-form thesis was an updating of Louis Sullivan's maxim that "form follows function." Pietilä's formula simply eliminated the modernist byword "function," advocating instead a more open-ended and accommodating proposal "form follows approach." By separating the idea from the form, Pietilä successfully invalidated the conventional notion of function as the controlling or dominant force in the field of architectural design. Instead of being limited to some functional response, architecture rather possesses and generates a set of more expansive, symbolic relations.

MacKay-Lyons's approach is consistent with Pietilä's, which treats the idea and the form as separate but necessarily related entities. The purpose of Pietilä's theory is to avoid the danger of losing the essential quality of the original idea as it is translated in the process of form-making. By keeping a firm grip on his notional ideas as he proceeds to shape those "well-tuned boxes," MacKay-Lyons is able to make a plain modern architecture. It is through its plainness that the original idea is clearly exposed.

In addition to his Three Fs, MacKay-Lyons has a number of other yardsticks by which he assesses a design problem and explores ways to tackle its solution. One of these relates to the impression a structure should give of its prevailing social character, be it prestigious or merely modest. Of course, our architect allows that these diverse qualities may be combined in the one building, where a "modest exterior" might conceal a distinctly "prestigious interior." In such cases, Brian describes the building as possessing a hidden virtue. The House on the Nova Scotia Coast No. 22 (1997–98) would-

seem to provide abundant evidence of this, its two tight box-forms nestled in the land-scape creating light-filled, exspansive spaces on the interior.

During the early, formative period of Frank Lloyd Wright's career, between 1897 and 1909 (a mere twelve years), the architect designed and built no fewer than a dozen notable houses. Six of these were built in the celebrated Chicago suburb of Oak Park, a community of well-informed businessmen and intellectuals who also constituted the greater part of the congregation of the Unity Temple, which Wright also designed, to replace a more conventional Unitarian church in the Gothic-revival style that was destroyed by fire. Wright's contributions ensured that Oak Park would become a model of suburban form and social expression that is virtually without equal in the evolution of early twentieth-century architecture.

Beginning modestly in 1897, Wright built the Isadore Heller House on a Chicago city lot. The major design problem lay in creating an impression of interior spaciousness within the confines of a very narrow site. It was in the planning strategy for the Heller House that Wright's genius triumphed. By developing a linear progression from room to room throughout the length of the site, he created a sense of spatial continuity. The result was a plan concept that continues to be a model for similarly restricted sites.

A series of houses followed that took Wright's prototype and developed it in various ways. In 1901 Wright built two houses in Oak Park: the Fricke House and the Thomas House. Between 1901 and 1902 he built the Heartley House as well as the celebrated W. E. Martin and Willits houses. By 1910 he had added the Cheney House (1903), the Heath House (1905), the Robie House (1906–10), the Coonley House (1907–08), and the Gale House (1909). If Wright had designed no further buildings,

this early flourish of domestic architecture would have established his preeminence as a modern architect.

Almost exactly a century later, Brian MacKay-Lyons has built a provocative series of houses in Nova Scotia responding to the climatic and material conditions of Canada's Atlantic coast, while at the same time developing an approach that embodies both cultural and regionalist forces in the expression of these house ideas. It is, of course, still too early to assess whether MacKay-Lyons's residential production has equivalent importance to that of Wright's domestic architecture. However, the parallels between Wright's early concentration on private residences and MacKay-Lyons's vigorous output of highly individual houses between 1995 and 2004 offer compelling evidence for comparing the achievements of these two architects.

First of all, there is the importance of the region to both Wright and MacKay-Lyons. The style or expression that Wright invented for Chicago and its suburbs, the so-called "Prairie Style," with the wide overhang of its low-pitched roofs, certainly had more affinity with the wide open spaces of the West and Midwest than with the prosperous and sophisticated suburbs of Chicago. Wright made reference to Oak Park and adjacent River Forest as though they owed their foundation to the prairie, but as the names of those suburbs indicate, their origins were rooted in the forest. Similarly, Riverside, Highland Park, and Glencoe—all of which came to include "prairie" houses—were founded on what were essentially forest areas.

For his part, MacKay-Lyons crafts more direct relationships between his houses and their habitats. He not only responds directly to the climatic and cultural elements of Nova Scotia, he also creates a series of symbolic statements and places them within the regional

landscape of his homeland. Thus, he literally plants distinctive evidence of dwelling in his native terrain through the siting of these quite individual landmarks. MacKay-Lyons is not practicing as a stylist, as Wright did during the early stages of his career.

This is nowhere more apparent than in the definitive statement made in House No. 22. Among all the MacKay-Lyons houses I have visited, this one is for me the most coherent and appealing of his Nova Scotia dwellings to date. In the central living space, contrasting views present themselves across three sides of the dining table. To the left and right, one overlooks the open landscape from the drumlin; beyond the head of the table, one looks out onto the constricted perspective of the farmyard and toward the barn.

House No. 22's complexity is not numerical; it depends not upon the addition of extra components but upon the interaction of its two principal pieces. It's what MacKay-Lyons refers to as the hidden virtue of a building. It garners its spatial forces and its formal responses into a *rondo* of variations upon its principal subject, sending echoes of its major themes back and forth with the persuasive energy of a string quartet by Haydn or Beethoven. Here, he plays both poet and peasant, allowing himself to be caught up in a lively tarantella: obviously bitten by the promise of a unique natural site, he is unable to resist the cadence and physicality of this dance.

An essential element of this rhythmic structure is the existence in House No. 22 of a fine balance of inside and outside. From the exterior we are only aware of two closed box-forms placed in the landscape. Once we are within this carapace, however, a number of previously hidden virtues are revealed. For example, the interior opens up into a generous expanse of exquisitely detailed and closely related living spaces. In addition, beneath the wrapper a compelling spatial continuity stretches from one container to the other, linking the two quite separate space/form elements together into a unified and transparent whole.

In House No. 22, this fine balance of inside and outside results from the essential modesty of the exterior, the formal statement made by two very basic and unpretentious boxes that are placed so as to take possession of the surrounding landscape. The somewhat banal exterior character is complemented on the interior by a spatial freedom and continuity that promote a sense of expansiveness and prestige—even luxury—within the limits of the house's crisp, confidently detailed, thoroughly modern framework. Economy of means, simplicity of exterior elements, and the pure exuberance of structure, light, and form that furnish the interior have made House No. 22 a milestone in MacKay-Lyons's oeuvre, and I believe it will remain such for many years to come.

overleaf: Distant view of Hill House from the beach

The Hill House (2002–04) takes its name from the fact that it literally sits on top of a hill (actually, the crown of a drumlin), abandoning all sense of cover except that of its own making. Wright would have deplored the siting of this house. He passionately believed that one should never build on the highest point of high ground; instead, he advocated hugging the ground at the brow of a hill, building around its highest point rather than on it. Wright preached that we should allow the architecture in the foreground to confirm, rather than blur, the supremacy of the high ground. In this way nature remains in its virginal state, inviolate and beyond the corruption of mere man-made folly. MacKay-Lyons, however, apparently chose to ground the Hill House on the very crest of a landwave, as though it were washed up like Noah's Ark on Mount Ararat, perhaps even casting it as a symbolic restatement of Pietilä's "Ark of Architecture," laying the *Baukunst* bare in all its plain yet sensual and life-sustaining boldness.

The Hill House clearly demonstrates that modernity is not a complete fabrication of anti-traditional attitudes to space and form. Here we have a traditional walled enclosure that combines the essence of a fenced farm with the form of a Roman atrium house. The enclosure contains the two classic farm elements of house and barn, the former functioning as the owners' residence and the latter accommodating guests. From the exterior, these two forms set within low boundary walls present an opacity consistent with the architect's confessed intention to create a private hilltop refuge. Within the courtyard, from house to barn, and out into the adjacent landscape, the project achieves a sense of almost total transparency that provides the owners with a virtually complete prospect of their surroundings.

The clients naturally wanted their home to be a good investment. They embraced high standards in terms of the quality of spatial experience and craftsmanship in detailing. Also, they wanted to use their financial resources to explore the realm of the aesthetic, to acquire an object in which they could live, relishing its unique and personal environmental attributes.

The whole process of assessing the worthiness of a house must inevitably include an evaluation of the degree of domesticity it embraces and exudes. And that, in turn, has something to do with the owners or occupants of a house. Traveling in my mind, I cannot now revisit the Hill House without including the ironic and witty owners as part of its being. Indeed, MacKay-Lyons's success in responding to the clients' wish list can be measured by the exuberant good humor and sheer pleasure with which these two professionals enjoy their new dwelling. Brian, for his part, found this pair to be ideal

clients, who knew exactly what they wanted and were always available and able to discuss its realization.

Nietzsche wrote of modern man:

> [T]he most characteristic feature of our "modern man" lies in the strange contrast of his having an interior to which there is no corresponding exterior, and an exterior to which there is no corresponding interior, which makes the whole of modern man essentially internalized.

The architect's mission is to create ways of opening up our internalized modern man, so that by inhabiting a therapeutic, plain modern architectural framework he may be freed to respond once again to the influences of the exterior world and the enjoyment of its culture.

Back at Brian's farmhouse, I pause in the doorway, looking out across the grassy foreground at the long stone wall that Brian has built nearby. The careful ordering of its quite substantial stones, although formidable in appearance at first glance, is on closer scrutiny resolved into a bold yet controlled composition of harmony and coherence. I ask Brian about the process of building such a dry-stone wall. He describes the gathering of the raw materials and the process of resolving them into an integrated and holistic expression:

> You have these irregular and unrelated fragments of material, and you want to make them all hang together. What you are dealing with is a random collection

above: Stone wall at the architect's farm

right: Plainness, the virtue of not competing with the landscape

of pieces of nature or humanity. They're all different sizes and shapes, but the job of the architect is to put these disparate elements together and make them into good neighbors.

It becomes clear to me that the contemplation of a dry-stone wall has analogies with building within this community of neighbors.

Whether it's stones or people, the ground rules are much the same. That's what rhythm and proportion are all about. What you're working with is the diversity of these individual components, and the design task is to bring them together into a sensible, unified, and meaningful whole.

This is clearly a job for the village architect.

The Howard House (1995–99) is an entirely different case from either House No. 22 or the Hill House. It is definitely set apart from the notions of duality and bipartite order. Instead it is formed in response to a single, driving force that stems from within the house and bursts out triumphantly onto a prow or balcony, confirming its nautical origins. The modernity here, although still essentially plain, is more directly mechanical in its associations, and the house form is, in consequence, more demonstrably connected to ship-building traditions. But the references are not at all indebted to the vague, generalized imagery of a Corbusian palette. MacKay-Lyons's proximity to the shipyards of Nova Scotia is reflected in the bristling vigor of detail in these more authentic assemblies of form.

When MacKay-Lyons and I crowd with David Howard into the prow-like feature of the house, the sensation I have is not unlike that which I recall from crossing the Atlantic on a Finnish freighter. Whenever the ship hit those giant ocean waves, its stern would rise up completely out of the water and the throbbing propeller shaft would send a terrifying shudder throughout the entire vessel. Like Messenger House II, the Howard House has a wedge-shaped form. Its monopitch roof climbs toward the south and a view of the sea. Significantly, Brian talks about the feature on which we are gathered as the deck, but the character of this cantilevered platform, thrusting out as it does above the rocky terrain toward the Atlantic Ocean, changes to prow just as soon as you abandon the image born of the drawing-board and step out toward the reality of the landscape.

Again, this bold approach seems to be a positive reflection of the Nova Scotia ship-building tradition that MacKay-Lyons knows so well. The spoken language of a ship

has to be heard above the bellowing and roaring of the waves; its sentences are formed and given expression by larger-than-life rivets and brass couplings and hinges and bolts and all things that speak up for the shape of shipness. There's no point in trying to speak in whispers at sea, so Brian raises his clear, vibrant Nova Scotia voice through these architectural details, making sure that it can be heard above the clamor of coastal rumblings and the thumping of threatening waves against the rocks. Against this East Coast mélange of landscape and seascape, MacKay-Lyons has forged his architecture to be "bold as brass" but in no way coarse or brassy. In this sense we should interpret his "plain modern" not so much as a refined version of modernism but rather as a distillation of the modernist tradition.

There is no question that Brian values the contribution made to design by tradition and by theories that have their origins in the evolution of architectural history. His ideas are certainly not exclusively drawn from territories positioned outside the boundaries of architectural culture. To the question "Can we actually identify any direct connection between Palladio and MacKay-Lyons?" the answer is almost certainly, "probably not." This conclusion is based on the fact that Brian does not endorse what he calls an "elitist, trickle-down view" of culture. He rejoices rather in what he labels the "democratic viewpoint," and this returns us to the importance of seeking out and exploring critical architectural ideas rather than slavishly copying pre-existent forms.

Brian talks enthusiastically about the essence of this democratic view of culture and the importance of its being generated through a grassroots approach to *Baukunst*. In reality, however, whereas Brian certainly gets stimulation and ideas from what are broadly speaking organic sources, through his education he is no longer confined by the intellectual limitations of a "pure" or "uncontaminated" peasant. If such a species

still exists, its members are constrained through an understanding imposed on their curiosity by tradition, which enables them to resist external cultural temptations.

In the most direct and simple terms, Brian is too well educated and has been too much exposed to the broad landscape of cultural extravagances to remain uncontaminated. Nevertheless, the realization of his own particular identity within that landscape is of great significance to him, and the vitality and freshness of his work offers continuing evidence of his persistent search to find himself therein. The landmarks provided by his coastal houses reveal his capacity to distribute that freshness in the Nova Scotia landscape—colonizing, as it were, his own terrain with his own particular new strain of plain modernism. The Howard House is a bold and shimmering example of the ship-cum-house, house-cum-ship of his plain modern architecture. In contrast to Le Corbusier's references to ship ideas in the Villa Savoy and other houses, MacKay-Lyons actually incorporates ship forms and details in the Howard House.

MacKay-Lyons is not seeking to establish or promote a standardized and identifiable form or expression. Indeed, the product of individual responses he makes to each site suggests the advantage of gathering the disparate and provocatively original expression of his work under a single heading. What unifies his architecture is not a recognizable style but a method of practice. MacKay-Lyons's overall approach is to provide his clients with a plain modern architecture that is inflected with ideas grounded in region and culture. From this position, from this identification with place, the architect has effectively distanced himself from both the irrelevancies of modernism and the excesses of postmodernism.

above: Platonic forms perceived in the landscape

right: Archetypal lean-to as "coast house"

Same Shoreline, Fresh Waves

MacKay-Lyons's "Three Fs" of architecture—fitting, framing, and forming—provide the essential theory for the architect's approach to locating and shaping his houses in the open Nova Scotia landscape. The urban *landschaft* is, however, commonly more restrictive, more enclosed. Viewed at a closer scale, the urban projects created by MacKay-Lyons tend to emphasize fitting and forming at the expense of what becomes the invisible framing of the urban edifice. This work also stresses substantial forms, not simply through formal substance but by endowing materials themselves with vibrant materiality. Importantly, this materialistic response to the urban fabric is concomitant with the appearance and rapid advancement of Talbot Sweetapple within the practice.

Beginning in 2001, the practice of Brian MacKay-Lyons has undergone a steady, persistent transformation that is moving the office forward with a change of emphasis. It is inevitable that most architectural offices engage in such a process. Following their inception, early success with small projects, and the need to increase the number of professional staff, offices expand their horizons, change their structure of responsibilities, and take on more people, hoping to attract a larger and more varied body of work. Also, in many such practices, the founder and sole principal seeks to grasp the opportunity such a metamorphosis affords to engage the support and collaboration of a partner. Taking such a step often involves locating someone "out there" in the wider professional community—a talented person to share the responsibility for growth and change.

MacKay-Lyons was fortunate to have such a potential partner already on board in his own office. As Brian puts it, he "didn't need to go out there fishing, because [he]

already had a good catch in the trout pool." Talbot Sweetapple had been a fixture in the office for some time but had played his part perhaps somewhat offstage. After interning at the office while a student in the School of Architecture at Dalhousie University, he was hired by MacKay-Lyons in 1998. Then at the ripe age of twenty-six, he served as the project architect for the Faculty of Computer Science Building at his alma mater. Subsequently, Sweetapple has served as project architect on the Academic Resource Centre at the University of Toronto at Scarborough (2001–03); the Canadian High Commission Building for Dhaka, Bangladesh (2002–05); and the firm's new offices in Halifax (2002–03). On moving into the latter building, Sweetapple—at the age of thirty-three—became Brian's first partner in the expanded practice of MacKay-Lyons Sweetapple Architects.

From the record of his responsibilities since 1998, it is obvious that Sweetapple has been steadily building himself into the practice. Brian describes this process as organic, referring to the "grafting of Talbot Sweetapple onto root stock." Of his new partner MacKay-Lyons says, "Talbot is the best native design student I've ever taught. But perhaps more importantly he is also appreciated by our clients and colleagues alike as an architect of impeccable intuition."

Early in our collaboration, Brian and I had discussed Frank Lloyd Wright's Larkin Building in Buffalo, New York (1904), as an "American Temple to Work." We later talked about Alvar Aalto's office, which clearly expressed the separation of the master architect in his own studio from the "slave architects" in the drafting room. We also discussed the studio of Norman Foster, where over a period of six years I joined the partners, project directors, architects, and staff, including Sir Norman (now Lord) Foster himself, in one large, democratic space, as I wrote my study *The Norman Foster Studio*.

The new MacKay-Lyons Sweetapple office draws on all three of those sources. From Wright's Temple to Work Brian has extrapolated the notion of a large, high, central space wherein most of the work is done, and in this regard he has also taken part of his inspiration for a democratic workspace philosophy from the Norman Foster Studio on its riverside site in Battersea, South London. From the Aalto model, Brian has retained the idea of separate "master" studios for his partner and himself, and suspended these at either end of the double-height Temple to Work. The view from a large window in this high room overlooks the rear of the site; behind the protective, in parts armored, facade MacKay-Lyons has created a complex urban fragment with the terrace standing for a "square" or "place" and the residential units completing the fragment. The office is situated on Gottingen Street, a scruffy, working-class thoroughfare that is reputably the toughest street in Halifax.

The great drafting table that runs virtually the entire length of the high room symbolizes the unified and chummy working atmosphere of the office, the very openness of the space expressing the democratic spirit upon which the practice is based. The scale of the room lends an aura of prominence and significance to the architects and their work—quite the opposite effect of the Larkin Building. Similarly, the positioning of the partners' studios at either end of the high room does not suggest a supervisory function for the their occupants, as does the verticality of the Larkin Building. As Brian expressed it, the partners' studios are strategically situated to be "within shouting distance but beyond spitting range."

Ship's Company Theatre (2001–04) is somewhat remote from the rest of Brian's work in Nova Scotia, and the two-hour car journey there from Halifax provided a fine opportunity for our further discussion. This theatre is an excellent example of the kind of public building needed to broadcast Brian's reputation to a wider audience, for it's a cultural object of a very unusual kind. It combines the advancement of conventional English-speaking culture—the culture of Shakespeare and the great heritage of English theatre from the sixteenth century to the present—with the culture of the Nova Scotia coastline that is invested in fishermen's yarns and sailors' salty tales of voyages from their native coastline in ships that carried them back to abandoned and forgotten shores. It was clear from our conversation, as we proceeded over varied landscape that Brian realized he had been charged with the creation of an *ikon*. This is not just a building idea that would stretch beyond mere appearance, but the realization of a state of *being* which would span between the world of realism and function and that of *myth*.

The idea was to shape the permanent home for a provincial summer theatre company that has for twenty years presented its brief seasons on the decks of the *Kipawo*.

This ferry had for many years traversed the Bay of Fundy until it was retired from service. Consequently, this cultural icon within the region plays a significant role in this project. MacKay-Lyons speaks of "treating the *Kipawo* as a ruin" that can then be sheltered "under the roof of a monumental but plain boatshed." My own translation of the architect's intentions is no less plain, although its interpretation suggests more cultural and historical reference than he has acknowledged.

Located in a lazy bend along the main road through town, this high-columned structure imparts an astonishing monumentality and sense of the classical to the modest town of Parrsboro. It is as though an acropolis has been lowered to street- and bay-level, while the old ferry is elevated in turn to float within the entry portico of the theatre. In this way, the openness of the theatre colonnade—which is immediately contrasted by the "closed" thick wall (in which the service and servant functions are concealed)—achieves an extraordinary presence on the street. The openness of the portico offers total transparency to the passerby, but this transparency is instantly denied by the mystical and defensive "thick wall." This dramatic contrast speaks to the essential duality of Greek mythology. Greek myths mix reality with those heroic dimensions that can only be experienced in a mythical *elsewhere*, in another world of symbol and heroics.

In Greek mythology, reality is portrayed as an accessible landlocked kingdom, which is contrasted by the necessity to undertake a voyage to a world beyond, to some far-flung and entirely unknown terrain, in search of something that is unattainable in the real world. This contrasted duality is also reflected in Greek drama and in Western drama ever since the time of classical Greece. The architectural form of the Greek theatre is, on first appearance, a construct entirely based on limitless space, open-air trans-

above: New copper penny

overleaf: Monumental porch on Main Street

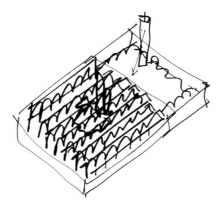

parency, where one is seemingly exposed to and can therefore see everything. But the *iconostasis* was invented not by the Greek Orthodox Church but in the Greek classical theatre. By this means, the drama or action is not limited to what you can see; there is also the dimension of what is hidden from sight—or, as in the Greek Orthodox Mass, what is behind the *iconostasis*.

The subtle achievement of the Ship's Company Theatre design comes from the architect's skillful translation of the theatre's interior world, which cannot be seen from the street because the "thick wall" intervenes between outside and inside. Instead, he has revealed a direct reference to the theatre's historical form by the mythical representation of boat and boatshed in the creation of an imposing, grand-scale, theatrical real world gateway to the world of theatrical artifice through performance. And magically, before we can negotiate the boundary between exterior reality and interior artifice, we have to walk across the deck of the grounded *Kipawo*, responding to an irresistible invitation for us to make contact with the actual performance space used by the Ship's Company Theatre during the previous two decades.

MacKay-Lyons's first building for the University of Toronto at Scarborough also provides an important link with the public domain. As such it forms a prominent component of MacKay-Lyons's new partnership with Sweetapple. The purpose of the Academic Resource Center (ARC) is to provide a state-of-the-art university library for the twenty-first century. In contrast to the Ship's Company Theatre, the ARC is functional rather than mythical. If it has a symbolic reference, it would have to do with significant scale, a reflection of the vastness of knowledge: an up-to-date echo of the great Library of Alexandria, for example.

above: Sketch of the Great Mosque of Cordoba

The new building is located at the very heart of John Andrews's campus of the 1960s and actually butts right against one of Andrews's brutalist buildings. In such close proximity, the ARC decisively distinguishes itself as a "well-tuned box" next to Andrews's crude, poorly finished *beton brut*, an inadequate translation of Le Corbusier's concrete forms and surfaces.

Andrews's buildings seem to offer ultimate proof that whereas Le Corbusier's *Unite d'Habitation* may exhibit a Mediterranean robustness in Marseille, the effect is totally lost when that vocabulary is translated to the less hospitable climes of Canada. What a relief it is, therefore, to find MacKay-Lyons's ARC, elegantly sheathed in copper and shunted right up against the unrelenting ugliness of Andrews's poor Corbu imitation.

Brian tells me that the inspiration for his ARC stems from his admiration for the Great Mosque at Cordoba in Andalusia. The Islamic origins in the form and content of his design may be readily traced to the Cordoba example. The first clue is the forest of columns that support the roof above the second floor, although the low-slung functional elements (known as "boats") that interrupt the vertical progress of the columns make it difficult to read the continuity of intercolumniation that had originally been the glory of the Great Mosque (probably the most extensive continuity of interior architectural space ever to be realized).

Following the expulsion of the Islamic invaders, a group of Spanish bishops prevailed upon the Holy Roman Emperor Charles V to authorize construction of a cathedral within the walls of the Great Mosque. Their declared purpose was to regain the Christian site that had been given to the Muslim conquerors toward the end of the eighth century. In reality they sought to permanently eradicate evidence of Islamic presence and culture. When Charles V visited Cordoba in 1528, he seems to have reacted strongly against the works he found proceeding in the Great Mosque, reputedly saying:

> *If only I had known what you really intended, I would not have allowed it. For what you are doing here can be found everywhere, while what you formerly possessed does not exist anywhere else in the world.*

Since our present-day experience of the Great Mosque is not vastly different from what Charles V found in 1528, I assume that MacKay-Lyons's inspiration sprang from both of these conflicting sources: the spatial continuity of the mosque as originally built between the eighth and tenth centuries; and the destruction of that spatial continuity perpetrated by those malicious Catholic bishops in the sixteenth century.

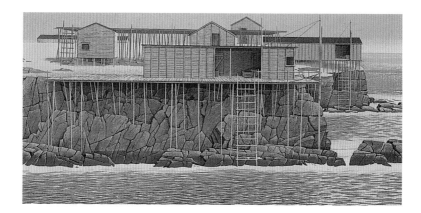

The forest of columns on the interior of the ARC certainly provides a strong sense of continuity and positive interaction of space with the structure. Through their simplicity they emulate the plainness of the original Umayyad structure for the Great Mosque.

The columns in the auditorium of the ARC are charged with supporting not only the roof but also the gangways that run along the outsides of the flanking walls: here the brackets that transfer the adjacent gangway loads to the columns have been embedded within the surface alignment of the column mass. Perhaps the plain modern solution to this problem might have been achieved by attaching the brackets to the finished column.

The outstanding success of the ARC resides in the airiness and clarity of the entire interior, created by the predominance of natural light. There is a sparkle in the overall appearance of the interior spaces, with their emphasis on material refinement. MacKay-Lyons has always emphasized the materiality of his buildings, but this has resided mainly in exterior treatments—the precise overlap of cedar shingles, for example. But here, within the ARC, the sheer simplicity of the columns, along with the craftsmanship of the concrete block walls (a low-cost alternative to Andrews's poured concrete slabs), are highlighted by the introduction of a traditional treatment—slabs of cherry-wood that seemingly float through the building and bring warmth and a sense of intimacy to this state-of-the-art Library of the Future.

The ARC clearly occupies a key place in MacKay-Lyons's transition from domestic to public architecture. As an architectural experiment, one certainly admires the bold confidence with which Brian strides out across this new field of endeavor. The

"Sheds in Winter," painting by Christopher Pratt

Grand Mosque of Cordoba provides a most challenging typology of form. Brian's awareness of the classical tradition, however, seems more reminiscent of Kahn's design language here than that of the Great Mosque. If the ARC design falls short of being a completely coherent statement, in its energy and provocative originality it undoubtedly bristles with promise.

The Canadian High Commission (the equivalent of an embassy among the member states of the Commonwealth) in Dhaka, Bangladesh, also represents an expansion of the firm's role on the international stage. The project stemmed from a national call for design proposals from the Department of Foreign Affairs and International Trade in 2002. Although the client is a Canadian governmental department, the commission is MacKay-Lyons's first for a site outside North America.

Reflecting on the project, Brian emphasizes its symbolic aspect:

From my very early days as a student I believed that the best opportunity to represent one's country as an architect was through the design of an embassy. That seems to offer the most privileged commission. It should embrace pride in one's own culture, combined with respect for the culture of the host country.

The challenge of transferring his contextual views and critical regionalist approach from one culture to another also excited him. The severity of the geography and the effect of monsoons on Bangladesh raised an interesting question of climate and materials.

When he flew to Dhaka, his first impression was of a landscape completely submerged under water. Situated on the Ganges Delta floodplain, the city relies on silt as

its principal natural resource. This results in an urban architecture built primarily of clay brick, made by a local labor force that is abundant, inexpensive, and skilled. The emphasis on modesty within the Islamic culture, in combination with a hot, tropical climate, generates an architecture centered on open courtyards. All of these conditions would be factored into Brian's design strategy.

In the tradition of the local material culture, MacKay-Lyons focused on the production of a sustainable architecture mainly derived from the use of local brick, combined with reinforced poured-concrete frames to provide earthquake resistance. Against this background of indigenous form and texture, metal skin and louvers were used in order to designate public elements of the project.

MacKay-Lyons oriented the Canadian High Commission toward the street and placed emphasis on its accessibility. Although its site is somewhat removed from most public transportation and local settlement (making it unlikely that pedestrians will encounter the building during their everyday lives), the design demonstrates an empathy and openness for Bangladeshi culture through its accentuation of the Islamic courtyard form. Brian stresses, "The social-democratic notions embodied in the building's openness are a natural reflection of our basic Canadian values." He notes that, even though it was necessary to work within DFAIT's design standards, he found it possible to derive the building forms directly from cultural, climatic, and local urban factors.

For the external image of this High Commission, MacKay-Lyons aimed at creating a "modest urban fragment" that had distinct associations with Dhaka and the city's immediate surroundings. Its material realization will draw upon the contrast between local brick and the metal skin with louvers that identifies the building's public areas.

The primary representational areas are the Immigration Hall, the Consular Foyer Atrium, and the Great Room of the Official Residence. All are finished in Canadian maple. A functional office building exists behind an all-important security line. Spatially, the hierarchy from public areas to private rooms is clearly discernable, while the circulation and way-finding within the building is immediately evident through reference to the interior spine of the narrow courtyard form. The courtyard embraces two discreet gardens: a public garden for the consular entrance, and a private one for the High Commissioner's residence.

From the evidence we presently have for the Canadian High Commission, it is clear that Brian's design concept is intended to offer a balanced blend of place, culture, form, and material. Indeed, as the architect reveals his building idea to us, it seems to refer back to his theory for the Nova Scotia houses, to the necessity for fitting, framing, and forming a building into the site; of forging an attachment between architecture and, what is here, the townscape. It may seem somewhat ironic, then, that MacKay-Lyons's most "public" building to date will be virtually invisible to the greater public worldwide. On the other hand, what Brian refers to as a building's hidden virtues will be fully visible to the residents of Dhaka, and is that not, after all, the purpose of an embassy, to represent the nature and interests of one country to the people and society of another?

MacKay-Lyons's "Three Fs of architecture"—fitting, framing, and forming—provide the essential theory for the architect's approach to locating and shaping his houses in the open Nova Scotia landscape. The urban *landschaft* is commonly more restrictive, more enclosed, and in closer proximity to the viewer. I believe the urban context tends to emphasize Fitting and Forming at the expense of what becomes the often invisible element of Framing. We shall see here that it also stresses more substantial forms, which it does not simply through formal substance but by endowing materials themselves with a vibrant materiality. We can observe this in all of Brian's public buildings executed to date, but perhaps most forcefully, in the Faculty of Computer Science, at Dalhousie University in Halifax and the Academic Resource Centre for the University of Toronto at Scarborough; the metal-clad High Commission in Dhaka promises to exhibit similar qualities.

This more emphatic materialistic response to the urban context is concomitant with MacKay-Lyons's developing practice. What was already a taut and finely balanced interplay between structure (Framing) and skin (Forming) has now been transformed into a much greater tension between frame and surface. This may be understood as the architect's thoughtful refinement of the forming and wrapping of these more complex urban works.

As we have observed, the art of building that informs Brian's work is one that is passed from generation to generation: an established tradition, which underlies and reinforces the processes of planning, spatial organization, and construction. Clearly, this village architect works within such an established tradition, and within the implied security and constraints of its regional agendas. But if the village architect begins to wander abroad, beyond the restrictive boundaries of his village tradition, then he has to adjust himself to the terrain of a wider neighborhood, and to the complex urban world that forms part of an expanded region both physically and culturally. Having taken those steps to free himself from the limits of his village world, he will find himself now on a new plain of opportunity. At the same time, however, he will probably find himself less secure in his traditional beliefs, as he confronts the wider intellectual landscape of theory. Of course, the pure "village architect" is hard to find today. We have seen that MacKay-Lyons, like others coming from a strong tradition, has through formal architectural education already been dipped in theory, baptised in a faith that blends new beliefs with the old ones.

At this point in Brian's career, at the beginning of the twenty-first century and as he now crosses the threshold into truly international practice, the increasing value of these distinguishing characteristics in his work is being established by the vitality of both the architect's ideas and his forms. Brian himself makes the distinction between the "village architect" and the "international architect," and the commission to design the Canadian High Commission building for Dhaka, Bangladesh, has decidedly carried him physically over the threshold between the village—for which we should read "region" here— and the big, wide world of international practice. At the same time, we should recognize that it was the international quality of Brian's village work—especially the virtues of his exceptional regional houses for his native Nova Scotia—that brought him to the attention of a multi-national audience of discriminating admirers.

above: Bangladeshi brick

overleaf: Northern lights from the Danielson House

(1996–98) Barn House

Upon my return to Nova Scotia in 1983 after several years of studying, working, and living abroad in Kyoto, Los Angeles, and Siena, I made the choice to study the landscape and building traditions that I had grown up with, in order to develop a modern architectural language that would be connected to place. The discipline of "seeing," in the sense that John Berger uses it in his book *Ways of Seeing*, would then be transferable to an international practice. This would involve a deliberate process of progressive abstraction, beginning with local vernacular building forms. The resulting projects illustrate some of the fruits of this journey; like a trail of bread crumbs left in the woods, they enable me to find my way home.

The Barn House is one of many projects periodically undertaken by my practice that returns to quote a traditional gabled form. These quiet projects, affectionately referred to by my colleague Talbot as "B-sides," knit almost invisibly into their rural and urban contexts as good neighbors. They allow us to refresh ourselves by "going home" to the sources of inspiration for the practice.

The Barn House employs the formal typology of the English barn and recalls an historic structure that stood across the road but was demolished in the early 1990s. In its reinterpretation, our project exaggerates, attenuates, distills, idealizes, and elementalizes its design precedent. For example, the generous roof overhang is 12 feet wide, whereas the metal roof edge is reduced to a thickness of just 3 inches. All trim is removed, resulting in minimal, woven cedar-shingled corners. The eight flanking pavilions

are expressed as discreet elements; transparent, they are permeated by the southern sun and the northern ocean view.

From a material culture perspective, the tectonic expression of the house celebrates the wooden shipbuilding traditions of Nova Scotia. The 35-foot—tall great room creates the impression of an overturned boat hull, supported on eight "chalks" for the winter—a haunting image from my childhood. The glulam "ribs," the longitudinal "keel," and the round double "masts" with their lanterns all interlock structurally, as in the construction of a wooden vessel. The chalks are designed to house life-sized folk-art figures, which guard this templelike pavilion. The great room is flanked at either end by totemic hearth and kitchen. Private spaces are accommodated behind, in shedlike additions.

Abstracted barn in the forest

left: A filter in the landscape
right: Thematic detail

Approach to the front door

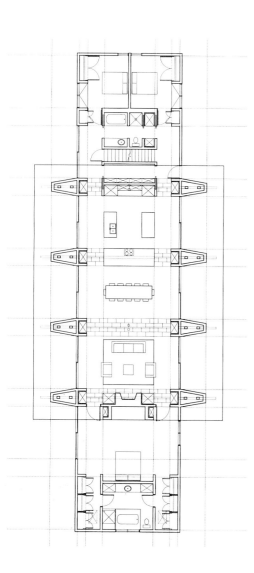

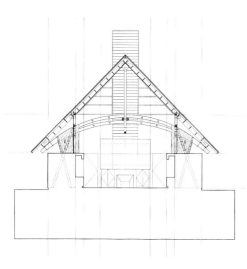

top: Ground plan
bottom: Latitudinal section

left: Precedent
right: Prefabricated elements meet up at the site

left: Great hall guarded by folk art figures
right: Hearth

Pavilion in the woods

(1995–97) House on the Nova Scotia Coast No. 12

This house, which consists of two primary forms—a mute retaining wall building containing the garage that runs parallel to the sea and a living pavilion that intersects it at a 90-degree angle—creates a microclimate that supports a south-facing garden. The entry occurs at the juncture of these forms, along a visual axis on the site that aligns with a pre-existing wharf. Although constructed before the Howard House, Coast House No. 12 was designed afterward, with a larger and more complex program and a more challenging slope and site. Both houses, however, mark the evolution within the practice of a "cross-grain" coast house type. Ultimately derived from the vernacular fishing shed, these houses are oriented perpendicular to the coastline and to the slope of the land as it approaches the sea. The result is a shiplike feeling and a sense of the house being aloft. This effect is achieved through the treatment of the building's section, by creating a continuous open tube on the main level that reaches out to the sea. Cellular spaces are tucked below, and the master bedroom and a study loft are located above.

The desire for this modern, free section drove the tectonic expression of the house. In wood-frame construction, resisting vertical gravity loads is simple, but resisting horizontal wind loads is difficult, due to the challenge of creating tension

connections in wood. In Coast House No. 12, wind loads were resolved through the creation of a series of four wind shear frames across the narrow 16-foot transverse axis. Wind loads are transferred through wind trusses into plywood-clad buttresses and into the ground. Through this project, and through others such as Ghost III, which was designed as a didactic wind tube, I have learned to visualize the dynamic wind loads moving through all of our houses as if by employing infrared photography.

The shingled wrapper of Coast House No. 12 tells a story of the value of working within an established building tradition. The cedar-shingled skin is perfectly executed, with its four layers of shingles, 4 inches to-the-weather exposure, and its hand-planed woven corners. The spacing of the shingles is utterly uniform: no shingle has been "storey-poled" to fit around windows or doors. This zero-detailed skin that wraps the structure points to a northern-climate modernism, rather than the warm-climate approach normally associated with the movement. In Nova Scotia, where shingling is a dominant trade, Coast House No. 12 was shingled by a teenager for about Can.$10 per hour. In any other place the workmanship would not be as good, regardless of cost. Working within a deep seam of material culture allows the architect to deliver more value to the client.

left: Monumentality of modest means
right: Garden courtyard microclimate

Entry porch frames the sea

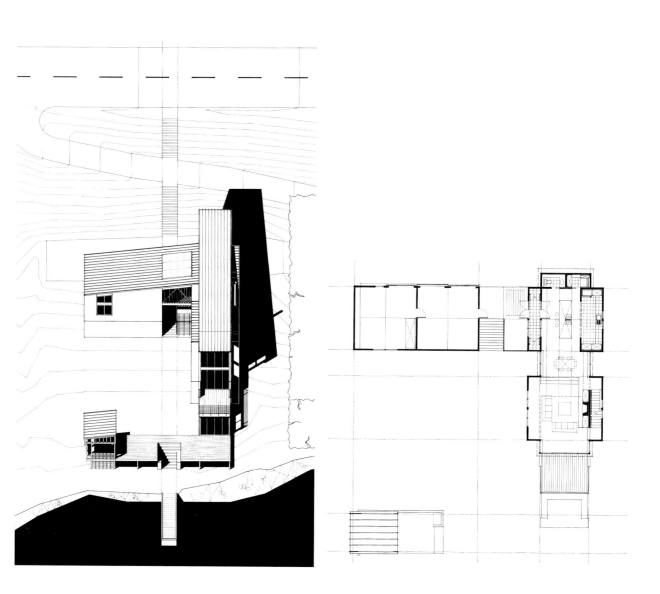

left: Axonometric drawing
right: Main-floor plan

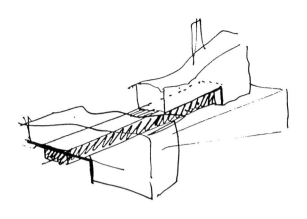

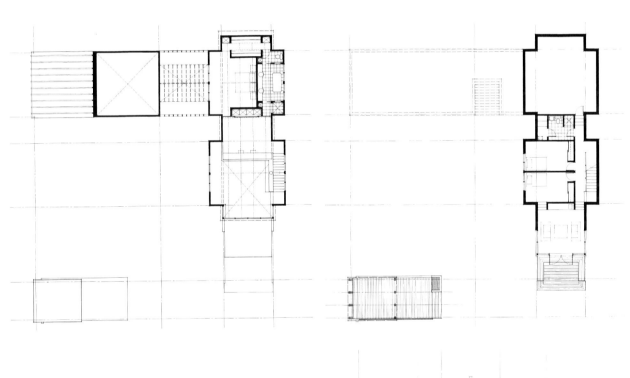

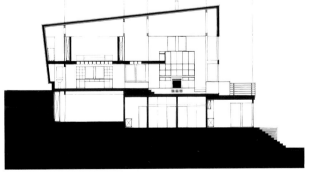

top: Initial sketch
center left: Upper-floor plan
center right: Ground-floor plan
bottom: Longitudinal section

left: Monumental great room
right: Kitchen island

Extroverted sea face

(1996–98) Danielson House

In Atlantic Canada we are "mortgage-averse"—reluctant to spend money we don't have. This has led to a pay-as-you-go building culture. Living in a tar-papered basement until framing materials are paid for is considered a sign of high moral fiber. Each year our practice has designed an extremely frugal project (in this case, under U.S.$100,000) in order to keep our work accessible and of our culture. When Esther and Bill Danielson requested a phased house, I was delighted for the chance to express this cultural ethic.

Phase One of the project was largely prefabricated six hours away, in Halifax, and then assembled on-site in order to cope with the short construction season and offset the high costs connected with building on a remote site. Over the years we continue to provide details for upgrading, insulating, and finishing this initially raw structure.

The house sits on the edge of a cliff on Cape Breton Island, at the northernmost end of the Appalachians. It looks out on the dramatic weather, the North Star, and, on a clear day, Newfoundland. Esther is a landscape architect and Bill is a weatherman; the project was thus conceived as a 125-foot–long landscape- and weather-viewing platform. The building's skin is chameleonlike, with interior and exterior sliding doors acting as "eyelids," protecting the house and its inhabitants from the harsh north Atlantic climate. In fine weather the great room on the main floor can be opened, dissolving the boundary between inside and outside.

The spatial and tectonic parti of the house is that of an archetypal lean-to, with a folded metal roof that inflects toward the sea. A simple, insulated bar building creates a buffer to the public road. In our social democratic culture, we don't put our family jewels, so to speak, out on the front lawn; as cultural historian Richard Sennett argues in *The Fall of Public Man*, impersonality in the public domain is necessary for public life.

North facade

top: Sliding "eyelid" doors
bottom left: Servant box with 24-foot sliding door open
bottom right: Servant box with sliding door closed

North facade

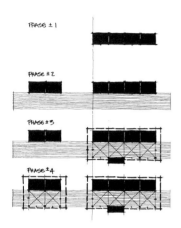

PHASE ± 1

PHASE ± 2

PHASE ± 3

PHASE ± 4

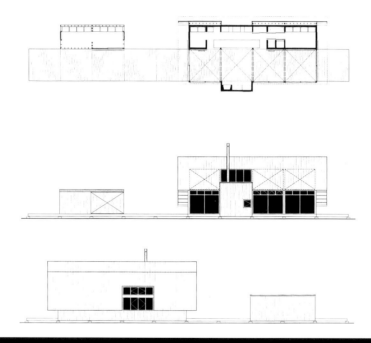

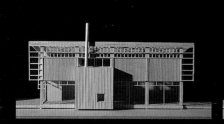

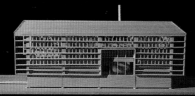

top left: Growth strategy
center: Main-floor plan and elevations
bottom left: Model from the north
bottom right: Model from the south

top: Satellite-dish shed used as precedent
left: Vertical sliding barn doors
right: Site assembly of prefabricated elements

Cliff perch

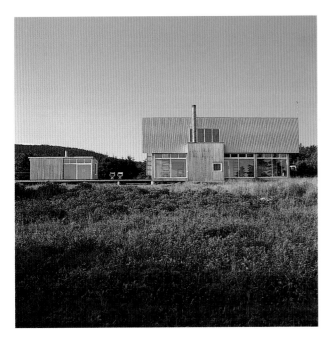

left: North facade
right: Esther's hearth alcove

left: Great room looking west
right: Great room looking east

House at dusk

(1997–98) House on the Nova Scotia Coast No. 22

This coast house presents an integrated response to the natural and cultural orders within the landscape which is also found in vernacular architectural traditions worldwide. Here it is expressed through the use of a highly abstract modern language.

This project consists of two structures boldly occupying two drumlin hilltops about 500 feet apart. Ever changing with the region's weather conditions, the landscape that occupies the space in between and beyond the buildings is framed from within. The main house enjoys a view of a settlement located on a river estuary, while the guest house claims a direct view of the ocean. The two cleared hilltops are separated by a wetland that is cultivated as a natural wildlife corridor and can be crossed by an illuminated bridge.

In the houses, the distinction between "prospect" and "refuge," to borrow Glenn Murcutt's terms, is expressed in section. The communal space of the ground level forms an almost completely glazed, 360-degree panopticon. The private space of the second level is protected within a Bachelardian attic retreat, which appears to float above the sensuous curves of the hilltops.

This house provides a clear example of what Malcolm Quantrill discribes as the paradox between the definitive, primary form-in-the-landscape from without and the indefinite spatial boundary from within. This dialog between external form and internal space is further reflected in the contrast of the more refined interior finishes of the polished concrete floors, maple millwork, and stainless-steel plinths with the rough-sawn hemlock of the exterior boxes. The internal elements are incorporated within a 4-foot groinlike void in the center of the plan and in its butterfly-like structure. This void forms giant roof scuppers, which return water to the cultivated wetland.

In both the main and guest pavilions, a rustic, muscular endoskeleton is wrapped with a diaphanous skin. When the fog rolls in, they float eerily, lanternlike, above their respective hilltops.

left: Entry lantern
right: Totemic spine

Guest house, reflected in plinth of the main house

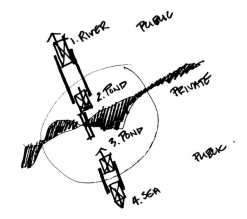

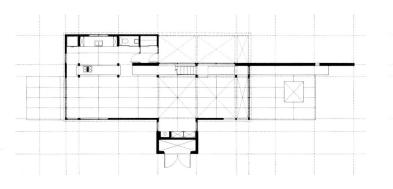

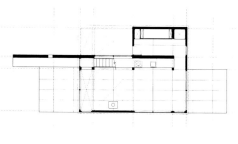

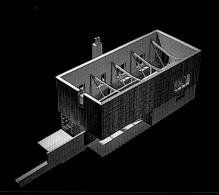

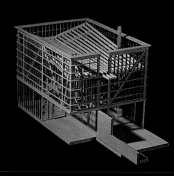

top: First site sketch
center left: Main house plan
center right: Guest house plan
bottom left: Main house model
bottom right: Guest house framing model

top: Range lighthouses as precedent

left: Aerial site photograph

right: Truss-filled box

95

Houses hovering above estuary

Dueling porches

View to guest house from main house interior

left: Main house great room
right: Hearth inglenook

left: Terrace by night
right: Terrace by day

Box floating above hilltop

(1997–98) Kutcher House

The Kutcher House is an essay on what Glenn Murcutt describes as the need for both "prospect" and "refuge" when dwelling in the landscape. The house hovers above a 100-foot–long granite boulder, high above the sea and the shipping lanes. It employs a protective archetypal lean-to typology similar to that of the Danielson House. The standing-seam, Galvalume metal roof folds down toward the forested north side, creating a rumplike gesture. The south facade is, by contrast, completely glazed.

Like most of our houses, the Kutcher House employs the feng shui principle of an indirect entry sequence, here heightening the sense of refuge for the family of five that inhabits it. On approaching from the north one is first confronted by a 120-foot concrete wall; the ocean view is withheld. On passing through an angle-iron gate, one arrives into the protected courtyard and leaves the wild, natural landscape behind. After "corkscrewing" up a scissor-stair onto the rock, the effort required to enter is rewarded with arrival to the serene, sanctuary-like living pavilion. The templelike great room offers an uninterrupted prospect over the sea, like some anthropomorphic landscape-viewing helmet. Much of the sky is cropped from view, thereby emphasizing the ocean's absolute horizon line—so much so, in fact, that when standing behind the 20-foot kitchen island, one feels that the power of the Atlantic might cut you in half at the waist.

The Kutcher House employs an elemental Miesian, rather than monolithic, tectonic strategy. Millwork, hearths, glazing, floor, steel columns, wood shear fins, concrete wall, and sleeve-like metal roof: each of the building's constituent elements is expressed separately. In this sense the project foreshadows a growing interest in articulating building systems that has carried through to our more recent, large-scale public projects. Both landscape and tectonic strategies support a passive solar approach, incorporating south-facing glazing in conjunction with concrete flooring fitted with a hydronic heating system. Hardwood flooring is peeled back in order to express this environmental agenda.

Protective north approach

top: Two-way roof framing
left: Sky detail
right: Angle-iron gate

Entry court facade

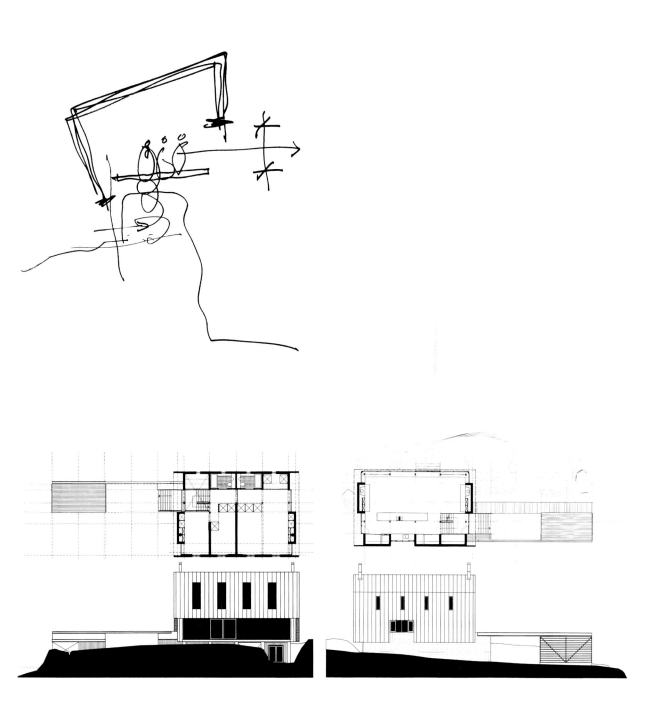

top: Initial sketch showing lean-to on a granite boulder
left: Upper-floor plan with south elevation
right: Main-floor plan with north elevation

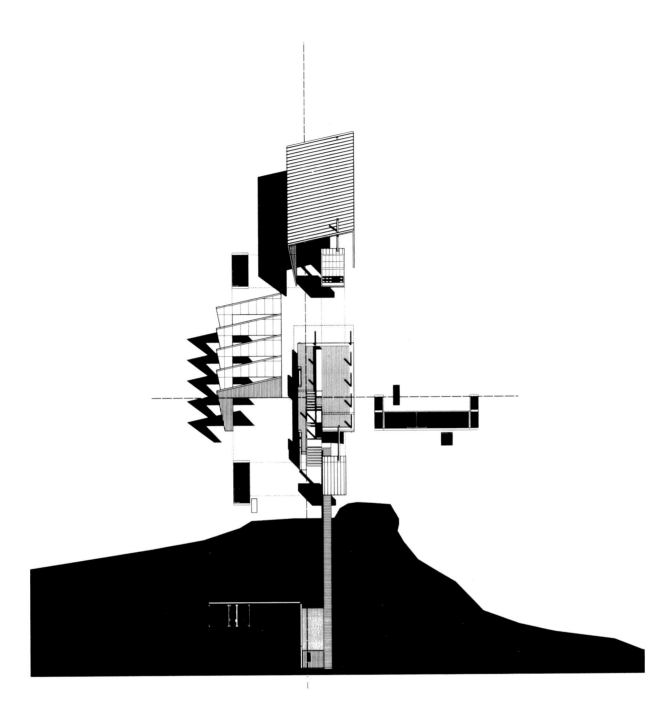

Axonometric drawing

Warm cedar entry gable

left: Gate detail
right: Ground detail

left and right: Miesian temple

Pavilion on a rock

(1995–99) Howard House

The Howard House was conceived as land art for an art historian and his family of four. It is a 12- by 110-foot wall that distinguishes the cultural landscape of the fishing cove to the east from the natural landscape of the wild ocean to the west. An absolute, horizontal datum running through the center of the longitudinal elevation renders the roof and ground plane mirror images. The east facade appears to be paper-thin and vulnerable, while the west facade puts its muscular shoulder to the wind with a concrete hump. The narrow, prowlike south end of the house fronts on the bay.

Glazing on the south facade and concrete floors with radiant heating form elements of a passive solar approach. The narrow plan enables natural ventilation. Sliding barn doors close to create a microclimate that extends the seasonal use of the courtyard. I am delighted to visit the Howards on a winter day to find the heat off, the windows open, and the children playing with their toys on the concrete floor.

Designed several years before it was built, the Howard House was an important milestone in the development of a modern design language for the practice. This language resulted from a career-long study of, and abstraction from, vernacular precedent. It is not a sentimental vernacular but rather the unselfconscious vernacular of pragmatism. An interest in issues of both environmental sustainability and cultural sustainability lead me to the study of plain and ordinary buildings. The vernacular is what you do

when you can't afford to get it wrong. Built on an extremely tight budget, the Howard House was initially taxed as a boat shed and valued at Can.$12,000: I took this as a great compliment.

The spatial parti of the house is a tube on the main level, with sleeping spaces below for the children and loft space above for the adults. This slippery tube sets up the problem of making places for repose through the use of totemic elements that provide focus (boulder, dining window, hearth-bookcase, south bay window, and south terrace). The use of a secret staircase, hidden behind the hearth-bookcase, pays tribute to my longtime mentor and friend, American humanist architect Charles Moore.

The house as link between the fishing village and the natural landscape

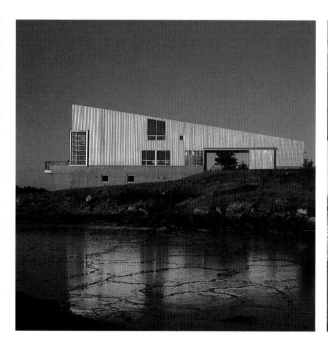

left: East facade in winter
right: The beauty of conventional framing

House at dusk from the southeast

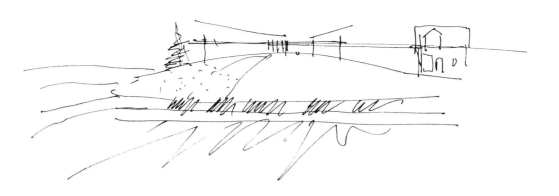

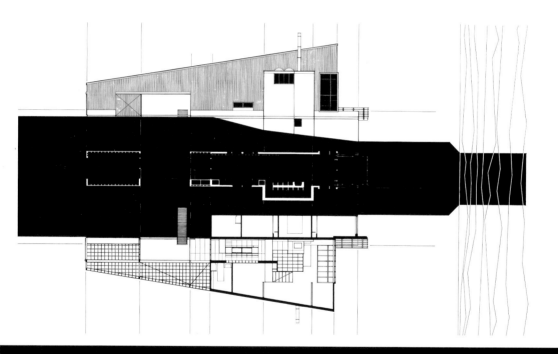

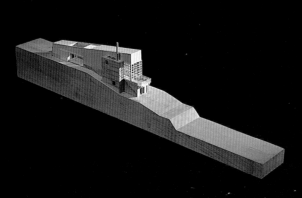

top: Initial sketch
center: Plan, longitudinal section, and elevation
bottom: Model

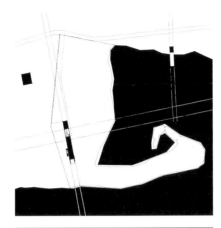

top: Site plan
bottom left: The unsentimental vernacular as precedent
bottom right: House under construction

left: Anna Howard modifying her microclimate
right: Porch framing the landscape

Monumental south facade

Passive solar strategies

left: Placemaking in a slippery tube

right: Living space from loft

left: A ship's prow
right: West elevation with protective concrete hump

The indirect approach

Messenger House II

Messenger House II sits on a drumlin ridge and commands a panoramic view to the southwest over the ruins of a four hundred-year—old agrarian settlement—a veritable microcosm of Nova Scotia's cultural history. Beyond are the LaHave River Estuary and the LaHave Islands. The simple wedgelike shape of the house is literally scribed into the curvature of the drumlin. In its radically monolithic shape it is related to the irreducible forms of surrounding vernacular models.

The procession through the landscape to the house is indirect; the dramatic landscape view is withheld until one enters the covered porch that separates the main house from the adjacent guest house. The northeast facade of the primary residence is solid and severe. The southwest facade is almost completely glazed; it runs parallel to an historic ridge road used for hauling sea-manure for fertilizer.

Messenger House II is an essay on traditional building practices that developed in response to the weather and weathering. Due to Nova Scotia's labile climate, with its frequent freeze/thaw and wet/dry cycles, I have come to see building skins as alive and constantly moving. The four-layer, eastern white cedar-shingled wrapper of this house with its woven corners gives an impression of a taut "shrinkwrapped" architecture. Like the Howard House, it utilizes sliding barn doors to protect both the interior and the courtyard from sun and wind.

The structure of the house is a literal expression of conventional North American platform framing. Not only is the floor the staging area for tilting up the walls but the section is identical to the plan; the floor is an exact template for the walls. The fabric of the construction is delaminated to explain its thin-skinned nature on the northeast facade, in the courtyard. It has a 70-foot longitudinal braced stud wall that bisects the interior; a didactic, tectonic device, it separates the house into what Louis Kahn described as "served" and "servant" zones. It also gives the seven-bay public area of the house a lanternlike cornice. A pair of cobalt blue, transverse shear walls that book-end the wall shelter sleeping spaces beyond. In this tight and frugal house, constructional order signifies spatial order.

top: House as camera, framing a landscape-format vista
bottom left and right: Two photographs (taken only minutes apart)
supporting the argument for a plain modern architecture

Object in the agrarian landscape

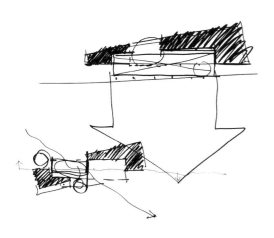

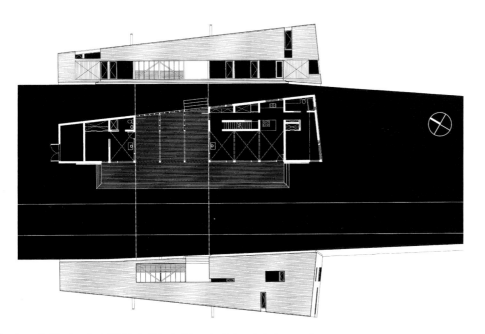

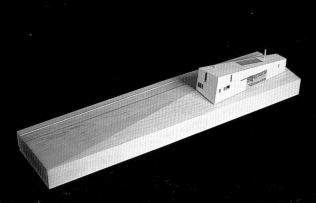

top: Sketch of the basic parti showing pinwheel (natural landscape response) vs. broadside (cultural landscape response)
center: West elevation, plan, and east elevation
bottom: Model

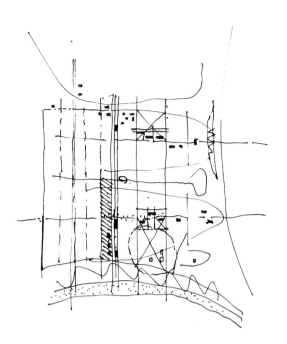

top: Site sketch
bottom left: Delaminated east approach with view witheld
bottom right: Carpenter's outhouse mimicking the language of the house

View out to sea from northwest

left: View to the west, revealed upon arrival in the courtyard
right: Drumlin ridge approach

top: Loft above the main living area
left: Cobalt-blue shear walls, bookending the public realm
right: Totemic studwall linking main house, courtyard, and guest house

Pinwheel composition, celebrating plasticity of light timber framing

Hill House

As its name implies, the Hill House is as much constructed as it is natural. Extruded from its bald drumlin site, the house is a landform, with its pair of monopitch roofs complementing the curvature of the hill in section. In plan, the house's midline traces the long axis of the drumlin. It knits itself into the cultural landscape by sliding in between a series of parallel agricultural plough ridges, or terraces.

Like many of our other houses, Hill House is primarily a landscape-viewing device. Like a camera, it frames 360-degree views of the natural (and cultural) landscape, here, for a landscape photographer client. This house commands the ultimate sense of prospect, audaciously occupying its hilltop like a panopticon. This desire for outlook, however, brings with it the reciprocal need for refuge on a windswept site, which receives the brunt of vicious North Atlantic storms. These two imperatives are resolved through the use of a courtyard typology. Two long, pinwheeling concrete walls create a protected garden. Both the house and the barn turn their rumps outward against the wind, while their glazed bites face one another across the courtyard. The relationship between the two structures ironically creates a prospect, through the interior courtyard.

Both in terms of landscape and a preoccupation with this material expression, the Hill House is a logical extension of a continuous line of research that has lead to a coherent body of work. It follows the "space between" focus of the House on the Nova

Scotia Coast No. 22, and it aggressively pushes the monolithic tectonic strategy of Messenger House II with its zero-detailing. A plain, rough-weather wrapper of eastern cedar shingles and local hemlock gives way on the interior to a warm, lanternlike quality. This contrast between inside and outside is both a climatic response to the vicissitudes of the Canadian weather and a material expression of our social democratic culture.

Guest quarters from the southwest

top: Barn porch defines entry to the guest house
bottom left: Abstract facade scribed to the land
bottom right: Porches frame the landscape to the west

View from the northwest

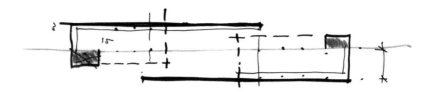

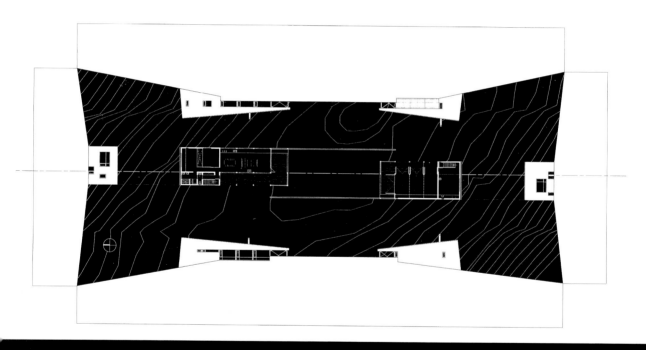

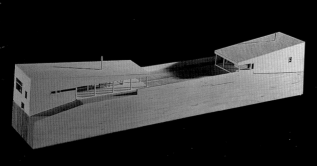

top: Definitive parti sketch showing reciprocating structures
center: Plan with elevations
bottom: Model illustrates monolithic approach to building

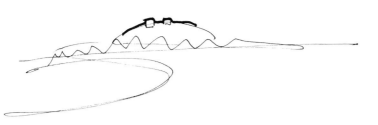

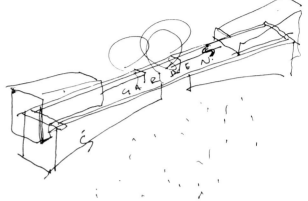

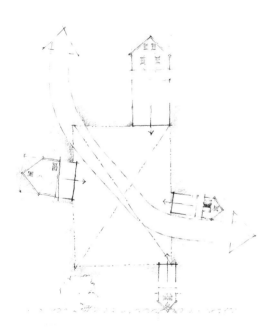

top: Initial sketch
center: Initial parti sketch with client
bottom: Sketch of the architect's barnyard from 1985
as precedent for courtyard scheme

East barn facade

left: Guest quarters
right: Study

left: Living room looking south
right: Living room looking north

Approach on a foggy night

Ghost Laboratory

As an architectural student in my early twenties, I quickly became suspicious of the nature of the architectural education that I was receiving. While daydreaming in the classroom and looking out the window at the life on the street outside, I felt a recurring desire to knock down the massive brick walls of the building and let the fresh air and sounds of the outdoors fill the Academy.

In 1994, as a professor in that same school, I saw an opportunity to take architectural education out of the classroom and into the landscape. The Ghost Laboratory has been conducted ever since, on the nearby four-hundred-year-old ruins behind my farm on the southwest coast of Nova Scotia. Initially begun in (1994) as a Dalhousie University summer studio called the "free lab," it evolved (by 2002) into an international summer internship offered by my practice, in partnership with the school. In recent years, the Ghost Lab has come to reside outside the university altogether. It has been reconceived as a nonprofit foundation and a loose international consortium of architectural schools and practices.

The Ghost Lab began as a critique of architectural education and is based on the apprenticeship model of professional education that has its roots in the medieval trade guild. This hands-on design/build experience occupies a position between practice and the Academy and, in our increasingly virtual world, has become all the more relevant.

The Ghost Lab is a test tube for research in the areas of landscape, material culture, and community. It feeds and is fed by the commitment to these issues within my practice. Each project acts as a measuring device, reading natural and settlement patterns through a built proposition. Each project is a study in light wood framing that is temporary, recycled, and biodegradable, endowing it with an ephemeral quality. Each July, the ghost is consummated and legitimized by a spontaneous community party and concert on the historic site, at the end of what always proves to be an incendiary two-week process.

Participants each year include students, architects, professors, and artists. Guests each year include a construction manager, a noted hands-on practitioner (such as Rick Joy, Bob Benz, Wendell Burnett, and Marlon Blackwell), and local musicians. Also, an architectural critic (such as Robert Ivy, Kenneth Frampton, Tom Fisher, and Juhani Pallasmaa) is asked to produce an essay, and photographers are invited to document the ghost's contribution to the larger architectural discourse.

Ghost I

Ghost II

Ghost III

Ghost IV

On the Fringes of Empire

Kenneth Frampton

This piece of land on the MacKay-Lyons's farm at Kingsburg, Nova Scotia, has been the site since 1994 of five successive ad hoc timber structures designed and realized by a handful of students under Brian's leadership in the space of two crowded weeks. Since it can hardly be seen as a summer school in the usual sense, it is perhaps more appropriate to think of it as a "hands-on experience," or even as a guerilla course in large-scale carpentry. It was, in any event, no easy ride, as I was to witness firsthand on the occasion of the topping-out ceremony that brought this latest Dewey-esque exercise to a dramatic close.

This event was the occasion for a musical evening, complete with a roaring bonfire fed with leftover timber scattered about the foundations of an old stone house. It was a setting out of *The Shipping News*, with unforeseen fireworks, firing off into the night.

Sustained by hot toddies and shielded from the penetrating chill by a motley assembly of ground sheets, camp chairs, and sundry blankets, the audience assembled before the improvised stage. Its elevated, rough-hewn boards supporting a display of local talent, the Blue-Nose Fiddlers, the extremely urbane Ian McKinnon, equally adept with flute and bagpipe, and finally, the guitar and voice of the heroic Lennie Gallant, all this to be played out against the restless presence of an impenetrable fog that permeated the land as it rose from the invisible surface of the sea. Was this perhaps the ultimate ghost, the deeper, older spirit of place brought into being by the music and an audacious structure, shining forth into the night?

The structure itself rested on sixteen columns at 12 feet on center, arranged in two lines virtually 24 feet apart, thereby yielding a seven-bay form with each bay being, in fact, a double-square. The fact that the land slopes from north to south—that is to say, from the stage upwards to the ruined house—meant that this underlining geometrical order was difficult to discern, with the height of the columns ranging from 18 feet at the northern end to some 12 feet at the southern limit of the structure. The columns comprised pressure-treated wooden telegraph poles, buried some 6 feet into the ground, depending on the fall of the site. These elements tapered from around 11 inches in diameter at their butt to some 8 inches in diameter at their crown—an *entasis* that was barely perceptible over the heights involved.

The inclined clear-span beams were also made of telegraph poles, with each composite beam, comprising two poles, bearing on 2-by-8-inch ledges. These double beams were scalloped around the columns, and the entire assembly was bolted together with 5/8-inch–diameter, stainless-steel–threaded rods with matching nuts and washers. The finished skeleton assumed the form of an inclined roof, running over a framework and hanging down on the ocean side. This grid was finally covered with muslin, bestowing upon the nocturnal ghost the character of a luminous wing or lantern.

Under the joint leadership of MacKay-Lyons and a local builder, Gordon MacLean, and with the help of Brian's friend, Arizona architect Rick Joy, this improbable structure was erected in two weeks by a group of two-score students, practicing architects, and professors. The point of departure seems to have been little more than a conceptual sketch by MacKay-Lyons, on the basis of which the students developed and realized the work. The first week was spent on evolving the joints, and the second was dedicated to construction. With the exception of power tools and the backhoe necessary for embedding the poles into the ground, the whole event was an exercise in pre-machine–age ingenuity, a literal barn raising that employed a block and tackle for hoisting the roof beams.

What may we now read into the existence of this quasi-permanent structure as it stands in isolation and unattended before the sea? In the first place, perhaps we should think of it as something more than a mere structure. In fact, it could be said that its ultimate function is to serve as a landscape marker; as a kind of sky-sign that echoes, in its diaphanous form, the equally planar outline of MacKay-Lyons's recently completed house for John Messenger, a building which now crowns the crest of greensward running down to the cliff-edge site of the ghost. The resultant space between these structures suggests all sorts of uncharted possibilities for the future, and this is perhaps the ultimate intention behind the gesture: the evocation of an agricultural hamlet that once occupied this high ground before the sea.

All this reminds one of another seafront settlement: the Open City of Ritoque, near Valparaiso, Chile—Alberto Cruz's utopian sand dune landmark of America, setting itself up in deliberate opposition to the gringo culture of the North. Surely, we are quite removed here in this reference close to Halifax, but possibly not as far as one might imagine, for the spirit lying behind this northern ghost runs wide and deep. There is a cultural undertow here that not so incidentally recalls the lost culture of the Acadians, brutally expelled from these shores by the British in 1755. Perhaps, despite our globalized world, this is still the mythic stuff of which some kind of cultural resistance may yet be enjoined.

Ghost V

Ghost VI

(1991-93) Faculty of Architecture Extension

This, the firm's first public building, represents a change in scale from the earlier houses, which necessitated drawing on different vernacular precedents. Here the agrarian, light-industrial vernacular of barns and fishing sheds has been replaced by the contemporary industrial vernacular of steel warehouses and shipyards.

This commission, resulting from an international design competition, consists of an addition to an existing neo-classical building where I received my first professional architecture degree in 1978 and where I have been a professor since 1983 (sadly, the only native Nova Scotian faculty member in the nearly fifty-year history of the school). This is a pay-as-you-go project. An initial (underfunded) phase boldly captured a large volume and continues to act as a vehicle for fundraising.

Louis Kahn asserted that the design of a school of architecture is the most privileged architectural commission. In this case, the aim was to create a building that teaches the architectural students on the first day of their arrival that the medium of architecture is the building industry: that a building can be seen as, and expressed as, a sequence of trades coming to the site. Each system (primary structure, secondary structure, tertiary structure, ducts, conduits, pipes) is articulated. The result is an

infrastructure view of the role of architecture—in this case, making a tough architecture that creates a place for the critiques and exhibitions that are the symbolic heart of an architecture school.

While modest in its material palette, the project is ambitious in its urban design agenda. Celebrating its position within the city, it formalizes a procession from the town clock, to foyer, to "new room," to the giant south window with its *brise-soleil*, which connects the school to the harbor mouth and the open sea beyond.

Both modest and pretentious, this building questions Nikolaus Pevsner's assertion that there is no connection between the basilica and the bicycle shed. It possesses an ironic monumentality and casts a more democratic view of our discipline.

left: Snyder's Shipyard precedent
right: Phase One, from the southeast

Metal box inserted into neo-classical brick building

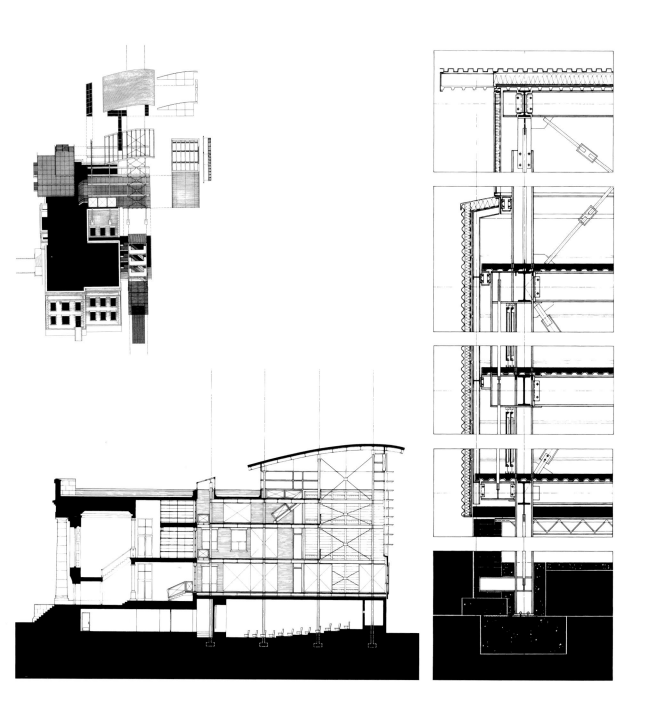

top: Axonometric drawing
bottom left: Latitudinal section
bottom right: Wall section

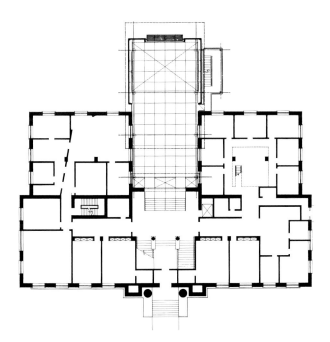

left: Main-floor plan
right: Steel structural system

left and right: Exhibit hall

Facade detail at dusk (Phase Two)

(1998–99) Faculty of Computer Science

In the late 1980s, the American architect Charles Moore said that the only architectural truth that he had discovered was that "participatory design always works." In 1991, my office prepared a campus plan for Dalhousie University together with consultants Attilio Gobbi and Giancarlo de Carlo (from Italy), William Mitchell ("on keyboards"), and Charles Moore (the self-proclaimed" Dr. Feelgood" of architecture). The result of a fully participatory urban design process was a plan unified by a linear garden and flanked by academic courtyard buildings.

Several years later we were commissioned to design a new Faculty of Computer Science building, which would become the first built expression of the campus plan. The project was executed by my firm as design architects with Fowler Bauld & Mitchell Architecture as prime consultants. This was a fast-track project: we began design with no site, no space program, and no budget, but with a schedule that required a fully occupied building in only eighteen months. This situation favored a participatory design process, which ironically proved to be a time-saver. It also necessitated a building-systems or infrastructural approach, where each building system is expressed independently to avoid interference between trades and to allow for sequential tendering. The participatory design process that followed allowed the building's end-users to provide the facility's content.

Dean Jacob Slonim's vision for a project-based learning environment led to the development of an electronic loft space surrounded by faculty offices. His view of computer science as an enabling discipline within a contemporary university led to the foregrounding of social space. A cyber café located within a 60-foot atrium provides a multilevel, interdisciplinary gathering place for the university and for industry communities. A social stair reminiscent of the one in Zurich's famous Odeon Café hangs in the atrium as an emblem of this agenda. As a result of administrative, faculty, and student input, the project challenges the stereotypical image of computer scientists as "male nerds in the basement."

The 200-by-80-foot, zinc-clad box floating on a cushion of glass spans a city block. Its thin skin is attached to a muscular, poured-concrete endoskeleton—a strategy often used in our house designs. The building forms a piece of the urban fabric that avoids image or style.

South facade

left: Oblique approach to the entrance
right: Zinc skirt detail

The minimalist, 200-foot street facade

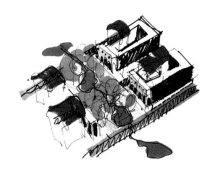

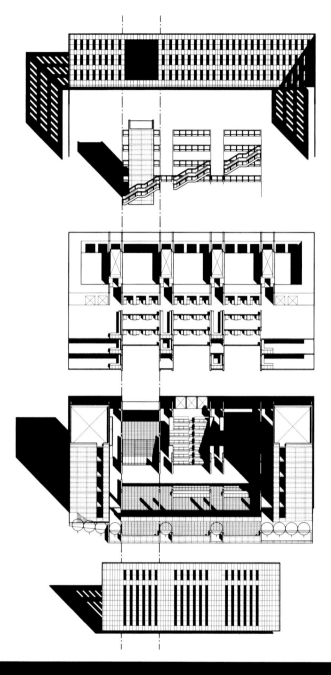

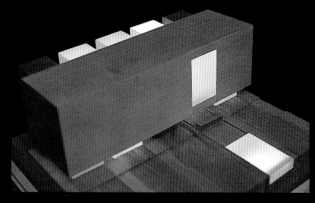

top left: Campus plan sketch
top right: Axonometric drawing
bottom: Concept model

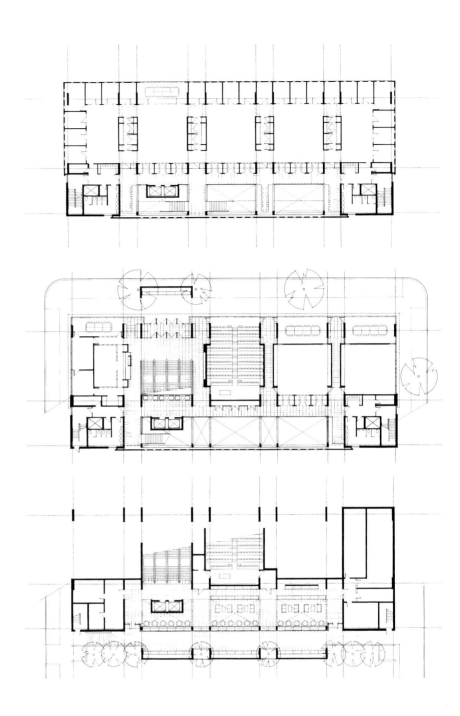

top: Typical upper-level floor plan
center: Street-level floor plan
bottom: Lower-level floor plan

top: Networked theatre
left: Cyber café from above
right: Foyer stair

Infrastructure approach

(2001–03) Academic Resource Centre

Located in the heart of John Andrews's 1960s brutalist campus, the Academic Resource Centre (ARC) functions as a town square and intellectual heart of the University of Toronto, Scarborough. A formal grove inserted into the flat tableland at the center of the campus, it contrasts sharply with Andrews's serpentine hill town aesthetic. It helps to urbanize this suburban campus by formalizing its principle east-west pedestrian spine and by defining a courtyard to the south.

As with the Dalhousie Faculty of Computer Science, the ARC benefited from an intensive participatory design process, led by our firm as design architects, with the Toronto firm of Rounthwaite, Dick & Hadley Architects as prime consultants. Jim Sykes, project architect of the original Andrews buildings, also joined our team as campus consultant. In this case, the user group, led by Dr. Robert Campbell, brought programmatic content to the project. They insisted on the development of a non-hierarchical space that would express the promise of the democratization of information in a contemporary library.

The resulting grammar began with a rational structural grid of concrete columns reminiscent of the Great Mosque of Cordoba, in Spain. This non-hierarchical structure is inhabited by five intermittent concrete block bars, which create a system of transverse streets and longitudinal double-height alleys. The alleys are sky-lit and contain hanging

steel bridges. The informally placed welcome atrium, foyer, five-hundred—seat theatre, networked study hall, and art gallery punctuate the plan with their double-height spaces. These social places are signaled by natural lighting and rich cherry wood ceilings, millwork, and furniture. The entire building is wrapped in a loose-fitting, standing-seam copper skin. A clear systems approach to the design resulted in a project that was 15 percent under budget.

New copper penny

left: Draped copper skin
right: Copper soffit

Copper entry sleeve

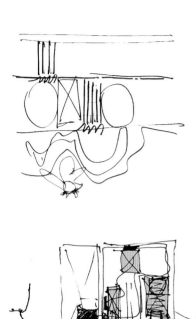

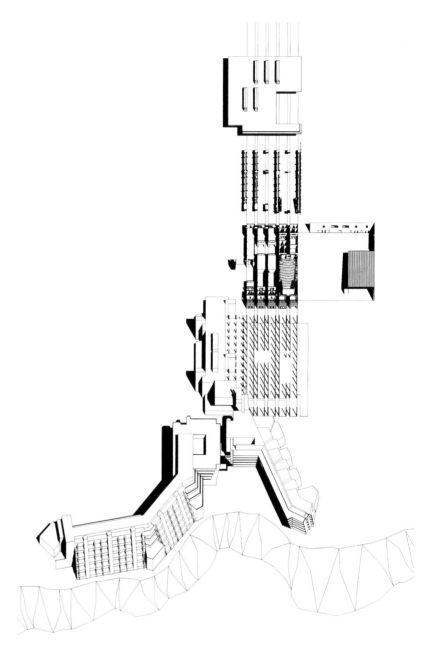

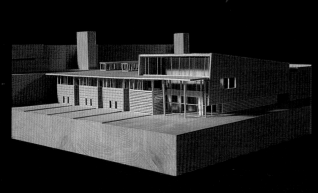

TOP LEFT: Initial campus sketch
CENTER LEFT: Concept sketch of public volumes
RIGHT: Axonometric of campus
BOTTOM LEFT: Model
BOTTOM RIGHT: East elevation

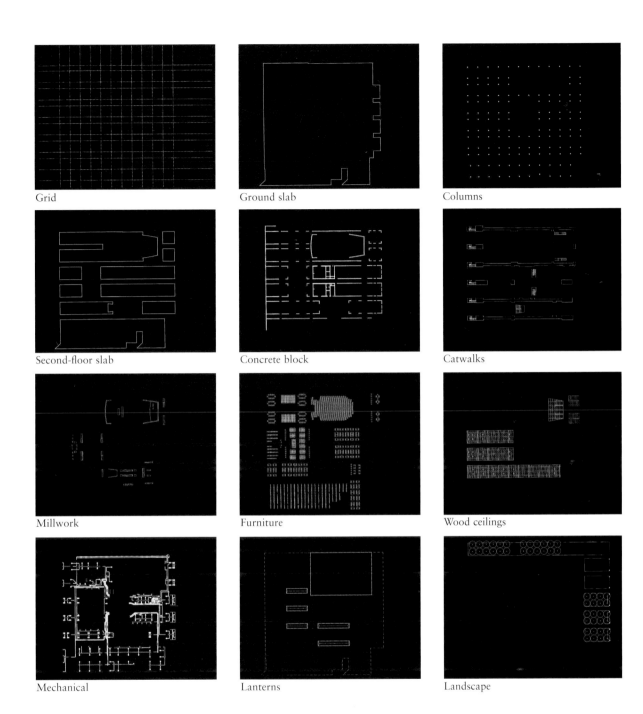

Grid

Ground slab

Columns

Second-floor slab

Concrete block

Catwalks

Millwork

Furniture

Wood ceilings

Mechanical

Lanterns

Landscape

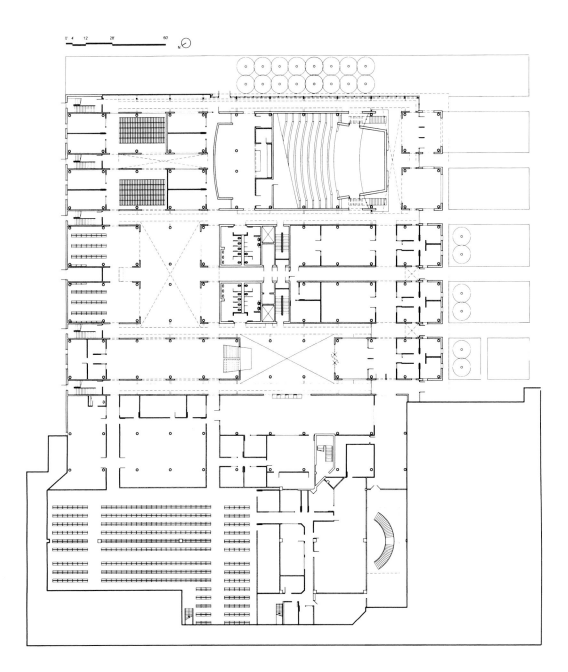

Ground-level floor plan

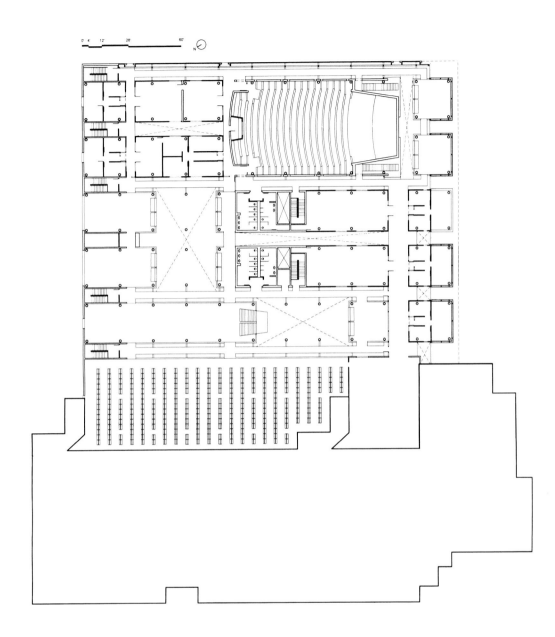

Loft-level floor plan

Typical sky-lit alley

left: Study lofts over entry
right: Seams, old and new

left: Five hundred–seat theatre, lecture, and concert hall
right: Theatre stair

Library arrival atrium

(2001–04) Ship's Company Theatre

For twenty years the Ship's Company Theatre sustained itself as a summer theatre in the small, remote community of Parrsboro, Nova Scotia, on the deck of a grounded ferry-boat under a makeshift tent. The constraints imposed by these conditions necessitated a creative response in staging plays. The beloved ferry, the *Kipawo*, had long sailed these Bay of Fundy waters, gaining the status of local cultural icon. It therefore had an important role to play in the new theatre.

A parti for the building developed through community participation. The ship was treated as a ruin, protected under the roof of a plain boatshed. The ship sits illuminated within a giant porch fronting directly on Main Street. The audience must pass over its deck to enter the theatre. From this monumental, open-air foyer one enters the theatre by passing through a thick, two-story wall full of service functions: box office, bar, washrooms, dressing rooms, green room, prop shop, exit stairs, offices, and sound/light booth. This wall forms the threshold between the real world outside and the imaginary world of the theatre inside. This new, flexible, one hundred and fifty- to three hundred-seat "black box" theatre noticeably contrasts with the original, constrained theatre-on-the-boat.

The location of Ship's Company Theatre is at the head of the Bay of Fundy, which boasts the world's highest tides. Forty-foot—deep mud flats or tidal deposits necessitated

long timber pile foundations. The free spans for the theatre were created through the use of a steel primary structural frame, with light timber infill framing. A cedar-shingle skin wraps the exterior.

This was an extremely frugal project for a nonprofit client group. The resulting architecture—the largest public space in Parrsboro—has a proto-public quality; like the missing link between the historical development of the local barns with their archetypal basilica plans and the local white churches, it builds on the history of the place. This plain yet pretentious building, with its monumental lobby and its minimalist, corrugated-metal rump on the bay, while modern and strange, is quickly becoming a source of community pride.

top: Foyer looking out
bottom: Public room from the road

Abstract monumentality from the Bay of Fundy

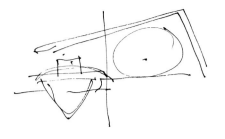

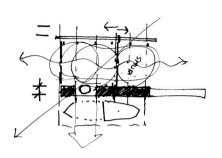

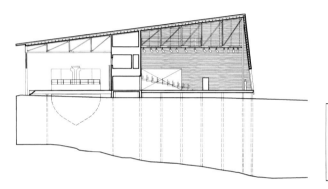

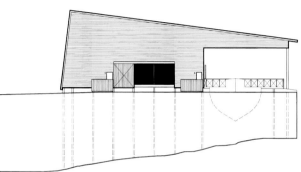

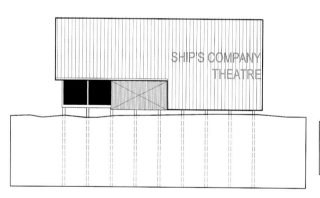

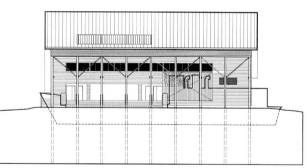

top left: Initial section sketch with grounded boat in porch
top right: Plan sketch showing zoning
center left: Transverse section
center right: East elevation
bottom left: Bay of Fundy elevation
bottom right: Street facade

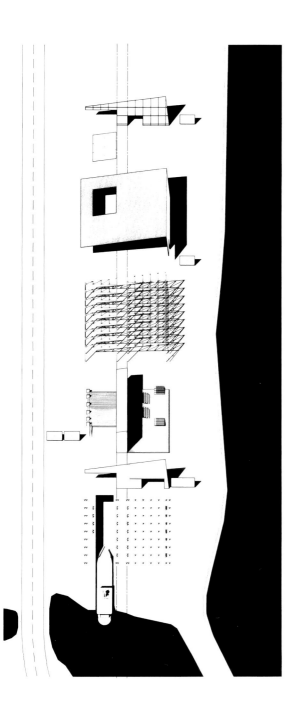

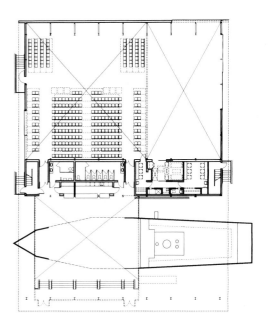

left: Exploded axonometric drawing
right: Ground-level floor plan

top: Ferry boat occupying the foyer
bottom: Theatre-goers gathering in the foyer

Reflection at high tide

Office for MacKay-Lyons Sweetapple Architects

(2002–03)

We have produced infill projects in this north-end neighborhood over a period of two decades, in this case (as in others) by acting as both architect and developer. The new office presents a tough facade on the toughest street in Halifax—a street that has not seen significant private-sector investment in more than forty years. This optimistic infill strategy has helped to offset urban decay and strengthen the urban fabric of this community.

This project responds to the needs of a practice that is in transition. In recent years the firm has slowly grown as the result of taking on larger public commissions, while still protecting the spirit of an open atelier. It has recently grown into a partnership with my able, longtime associate Talbot Sweetapple.

One enters the concrete block wall building under a 52-foot steel lintel, passing through the port-cochere with its 32-foot sliding steel gate and then into the southwest-facing courtyard with its recycled-granite retaining wall. All public spaces are contained on street-level: foyer, conference room, administrative offices, kitchen, and washrooms. Narrow shafts contain steel-bar grating stairs—the secret access to the hidden work-room above. While the foyer orients to the street at grade, this monumental "Temple to

Work" (24 feet wide, 80 feet long, and 20 feet tall) is oriented to the rear courtyard. Its focus is a central 40-by-8-foot communal worktable. Open lofts at either end contain meeting areas with breakout spaces underneath. Two-story maple cabinets bookend the room. Floating drywall kites both provide pin-up surfaces and shutter the 20-by-18-foot window.

This project embodies two important elements of the design philosophy of the practice: urbanism and humanism, or the improvement of the neighborhood and the celebration of the dignity of the work. The invisible nature of this building offers the practice a filter from much of the outside world, affording us a critical intellectual distance. Its tough, commercial, vernacular character expresses a plain modern, rather than minimalist, architecture.

Court with recycled granite wall

left: Pinwheel composition
right: Entrance foyer

Gottingen Street facade at night

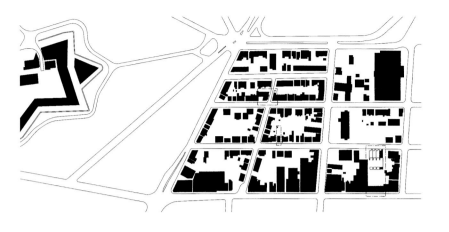

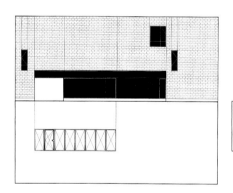

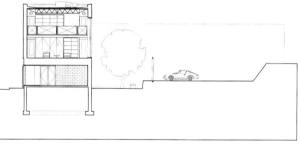

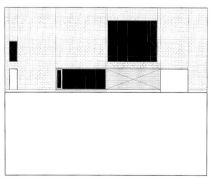

top: Old North-end neighborhood with sustained infill effort
center: Gottingen Street photomontage
left top: Street facade
left bottom: Court elevation
above: Transverse section

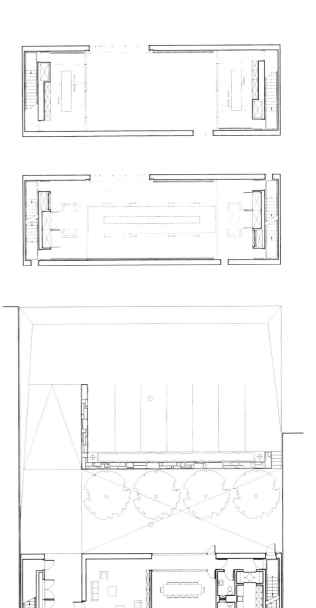

top: Studio-level floor plan
center: Ground-level floor plan
bottom: Loft-level floor plan

"Temple to Work"

left: Entrance foyer

right: 8-by-40-foot communal drawing table

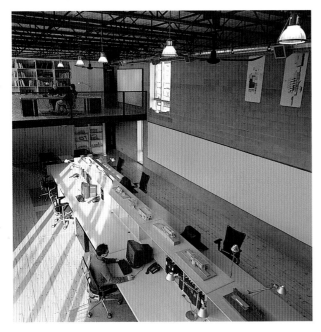

LEFT: Communal workspace

RIGHT: Loft area

Court facade at night

(2002–05) Canadian High Commission for Dhaka, Bangladesh

As a young student in my early twenties, I believed that the design of an embassy or high commission was the most privileged of architectural commissions. It offers the best opportunity to represent the cultural values of one's country internationally. Given Canada's domestic policy of multiculturalism, this project for the Canadian Chancery and Official Residence in Dhaka, Bangladesh, has a dual cultural responsibility: to represent Canada and to show respect for the culture of the host country.

Bangladesh is a country of extremes. It has one of the densest populations on Earth and is also one of the world's poorest nations. Its relation to the Ganges Delta makes it prone to natural disasters. One would have to leave the planet to find a natural and cultural context more remote from that of Nova Scotia. How then does an architect known for a critical regionalist approach operate in this situation?

My contextualist approach is not a style but rather a discipline, a method, a way of seeing, which is transferable. Building within the material culture or vernacular of a place not only communicates a respect for the building's regional context but it also maximizes the building's economic value for the client—an important benefit in developing countries such as Bangladesh.

This country is primarily Islamic, and the courtyard plan of the combined chancery and residence is a response to the cultural principle of outward modesty. This courtyard also mitigates the effect of the tropical climate by providing cross ventilation and shade. A monumental *brise-soleil* protects the consular facade from the harsh southern sun and signals the entry.

While our project is inspired in part by the monolithic masonry drums of Louis Kahn's National Assembly complex, an embassy, by contrast, is inherently not a public building type: the courtyard creates the illusion of a generous public realm, which is reinforced on the interior by three representational spaces: the immigration hall, the consulate foyer atrium, and the great room of the official residence. The Canadian Chancery is an accessible, welcoming building that engages with the local landscape and represents national cultural values.

The Ganges Delta has only two principle resources: alluvial silt and people, which translates here into the use of bricks and bricklayers. The building's material palette therefore consists of an elongated brick wall that wraps the courtyard. A series of folded metal elements on delicate steel frames punctuates the facade, reminiscent of the corrugated metal huts on bamboo frames typical of the region.

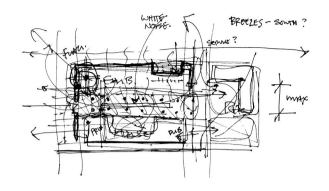

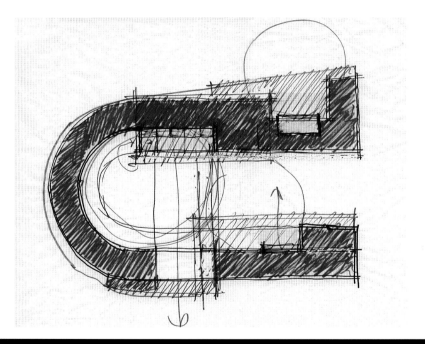

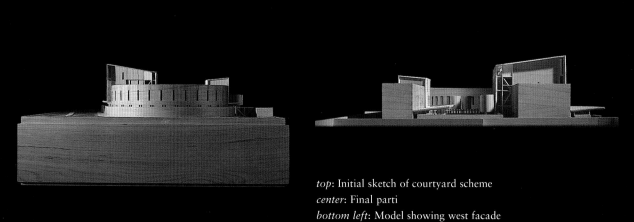

top: Initial sketch of courtyard scheme
center: Final parti
bottom left: Model showing west facade
bottom right: Model showing east facade

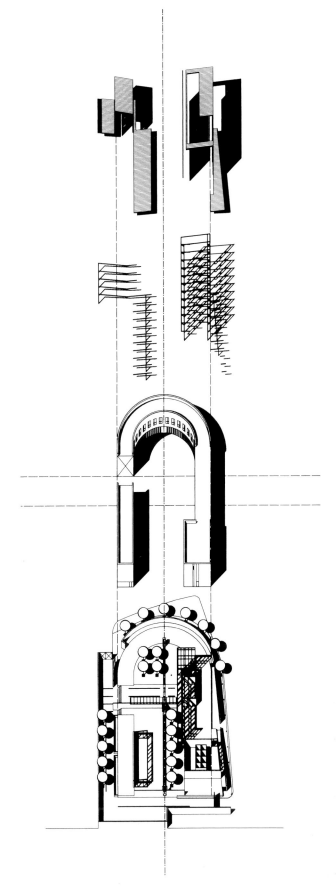

LEFT: Brick made from Ganges River silt
RIGHT: Axonometric drawing

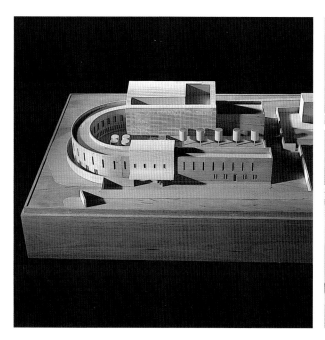

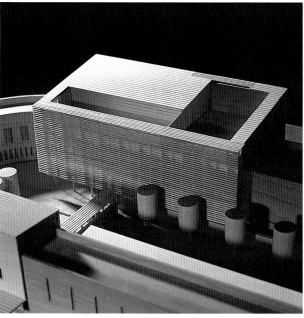

left: Model from the south
right: Model showing courtyard and consular entry

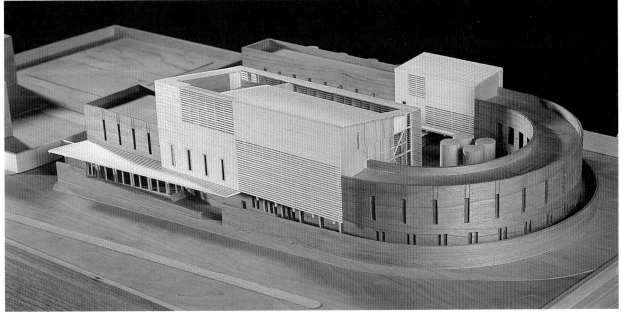

top: Perspective drawing showing streetscape
and imigration entrance
bottom: Model from the north

Project Credits

Barn House (1996–98)
Location: Withheld
Client: Withheld
Project Team: Brian MacKay-Lyons, Darryl Jonas, Trevor Davies, Talbot Sweetapple
Structural: Campbell Comeau Engineering
Builder: Andrew Watts

House on the Nova Scotia Coast No. 12 (1995–97)
Location: Withheld
Client: Withheld
Project Team: Brian MacKay-Lyons, Niall Savage, Doug Wigle, Tony Gillis, Talbot Sweetapple
Structural: Campbell Comeau Engineering
Builder: Cyril Smith

Danielson House (1996–98)
Location: Smelt Brook, Nova Scotia, Canada
Client: Esther and Bill Danielson
Project Team: Brian MacKay-Lyons, Trevor Davies, Bruno Weber, Darryl Jonas
Structural: Campbell Comeau Engineering
Builder: Andrew Watts

House on the Nova Scotia Coast No. 22 (1997–98)
Location: Withheld
Client: Withheld
Project Team: Brian MacKay-Lyons, Rob Meyer, Bruno Weber, Marc Cormier
Structural: Campbell Comeau Engineering
Builder: Withheld

Kutcher House (1997–98)
Location: Herring Cove, Nova Scotia, Canada
Client: Jan and Stan Kutcher
Project Team: Brian MacKay-Lyons, Rob Meyer, Trevor Davies
Structural: Campbell Comeau Engineering
Builder: Special Projects (Faisal Forhart)

Howard House (1995–99)
Location: West Pennant, Nova Scotia, Canada
Client: Vivian and David Howard
Project Team: Brian MacKay-Lyons, Niall Savage, Trevor Davies, Talbot Sweetapple
Structural: Campbell Comeau Engineering
Builder: Andrew Watts

Messenger House II (2001–03)
Location: Upper Kingsburg, Nova Scotia, Canada
Client: Mary and John Messenger
Project Team: Brian MacKay-Lyons, Trevor Davies, Chad Jamieson, Peter Blackie
Structural: Campbell Comeau Engineering
Builder: Gordon MacLean

Hill House (2002–04)
Location: Withheld
Client: Withheld
Project Team: Brian MacKay-Lyons, Talbot Sweetapple, Chad Jamieson, Melanie Hayne, Geoff Miller
Structural: Campbell Comeau Engineering
Builder: Arthur Baxter

Faculty of Architecture Extension, Technical University of Nova Scotia (1991–93)
Location: Halifax, Nova Scotia, Canada
Client: Technical University of Nova Scotia (TUNS)
Project Team: Brian MacKay-Lyons, Attilio Gobbi, Bob Benz, Niall Savage, Andrew King,
    Michael Carroll, Brenda Webster, John Geldart, Tony Gillis
Structural: Campbell Comeau Engineering
Mechanical: G. S. Ewert Engineering
Electrical: Strum Engineering
Builder: Dineen Construction

Faculty of Computer Science, Dalhousie University (1998–99)
Location: Halifax, Nova Scotia, Canada
Client: Dalhousie University
Design Architect: Brian MacKay-Lyons Architecture Urban Design
Prime Consultant: Fowler Bauld & Mitchell Ltd.
Project Team: Brian MacKay-Lyons, Talbot Sweetapple, George Coteras, Tony Cook, Niall Savage, Danny Goodz, Wayne Duncan
Special Consultant: William Mitchell
Structural: Campbell Comeau Engineering
Mechanical: Morris and Richard Consulting Engineers Ltd.
Electrical: Morris and Richard Consulting Engineers Ltd.
Builder: Les David

Academic Resource Centre, University of Toronto at Scarborough (2001–03)
Location: Scarborough, Ontario, Canada
Client: University of Toronto
Design Architect: Brian MacKay-Lyons Architecture Urban Design
Prime Consultant: Rounthwaite, Dick & Hadley Architects
Project Team: Brian MacKay-Lyons, Talbot Sweetapple, Rob Boyko, Dave Premi, Melanie Hayne, Momin Hoq, Justin Bennett, Kevin McClusky, Carlos Tavares, Dan Herljevic, Diana Carl, Dean Poffenroth
Structural: Peter Sheffield & Associates
Mechanical: Keen Engineering
Electrical: Hidi Rae Consulting Engineers
Builder: Walter Construction

Ship's Company Theatre (2001–04)
Location: Parrsboro, Nova Scotia, Canada
Client: Ship's Company Theatre Society
Project Team: Brian MacKay-Lyons, Peter Blackie, Trevor Davies, Naomi Frangos, Chad Jamieson
Structural: Campbell Comeau Engineering
Mechanical: Morris and Richard Consulting Engineers Ltd.
Electrical: Morris and Richard Consulting Engineers Ltd.
Builder: Fowler Construction Services

Office for MacKay-Lyons Sweetapple Architects Ltd. (2002–03)
Location: Halifax, Nova Scotia, Canada
Client/Developer: Marilyn MacKay-Lyons
Project Team: Brian MacKay-Lyons, Talbot Sweetapple, Vincent van den Brink, Naomi Frangos, Mark Upton
Structural: Campbell Comeau Engineering
Mechanical: Morris and Richard Consulting Engineers Ltd.
Electrical: Morris and Richard Consulting Engineers Ltd.
Builder: Fitzgerald and Snow

Canadian High Commission, Dhaka (2002–05)
Location: Dhaka, Bangladesh
Client: Department of Foreign Affairs and International Trade
Design Architect: Brian MacKay-Lyons Architect Ltd.
Prime Consultant: Rounthwaite, Dick and Hadley Architects
Project Team: Brian MacKay-Lyons, Talbot Sweetapple, Rob Boyko, Momin Hoq, Melanie Hayne, Sanjoy Pal, Dan Herljevic, Martin Patriquin, Justin Bennett
Structural: Development Design Consultants
Mechanical: Development Design Consultants
Electrical: Development Design Consultants
Builder: SPCL-GBBL Joint Venture

Illustration Credits